MAKING

CHOICES

MAKING CHOICES

THE JOY OF A COURAGEOUS LIFE

ALEXANDRA STODDARD

WILLIAM MORROW AND COMPANY, INC.
New York

It is the policy of William Morrow and Company, Inc.,
and its imprints and affiliates, recognizing the importance
of preserving what has been written, to print the books
we publish on acid-free paper, and we exert our best efforts to that end.

Library of Congress Cataloging-in-Publication Data
Stoddard, Alexandra.
    Making choices : the joy of a courageous life /
Alexandra Stoddard.
        p.   cm.
    ISBN 0–688–10935–7
    1. Conduct   of   life. 2. Stoddard,   Alexandra.
I. Title.
BJ1581.2.S7555   1994
170'.44—dc20   93–23921
                                                    CIP

Printed in the United States of America

First Edition

1 2 3 4 5 6 7 8 9 10

BOOK DESIGN BY MARYSARAH QUINN

To Carl Brandt,
my friend
for three decades.
Thank you
for your advice
and vision.

Love, Sandie

CONTENTS

focusing on and trying to make some sense out of what has happened so far on my journey; that is, I feel, the only way I can anticipate what will come next.

What I have come to see is that no matter how tough life can be, we can always keep our balance by concentrating on the choices that face us. It is always possible to choose, but being strong enough to do so is never up to anybody but us.

Until now, I've been writing about beauty and design, about rituals, ceremonies, and celebrations. I've rarely come out and addressed directly some of the hard issues we all have to confront from time to time. Though I have always emphasized the positive and fully intend to keep affirming it, with maturity I've also become acutely aware of the pain and suffering we each experience. These are the topics I feel I have to write about now.

Over the years, I have been privileged to find warm and extraordinarily articulate readers. I am at once grateful for and stunned by the volume of mail I receive—thousands of letters a year. I am continually amazed that by corresponding with people I know only through letters I have come into contact with thousands of kindred spirits, soul mates whose deepest values I share. Every letter is written by a person to whom I feel very close, and I read each of them with reverence. What my readers tell me has had a profound effect on my thinking and, in turn, on what I write.

With each letter I read, I wonder why a perfect stranger, someone who knows me only through my books, would write to me with intimate details of both the great joy and the great pain and anguish he or she has gone through. More than that, I am fascinated by the fact that there is rarely an ounce of self-pity in any of the letters I get. Since I turned fifty I have been spending more and more time reading and rereading the stories my readers tell me, opening myself up to them, seeing how they supplement and confirm my own life experiences, and gradually the answer has become clearer to me. I admire the courage and bravery that my readers have displayed in their own lives; they, in turn, find an echo, an affirmation, in the philosophy I have expressed, sometimes without really knowing it, in my books.

We all face struggles and conflicts, and we all want to deal with them courageously, with what Hemingway called "grace under pressure." This is what is expressed over and over again in all these wonderful letters. Together, my books and the letters I receive are determined to affirm and confirm the necessity of living our lives with as much vitality and intensity as is humanly possible.

I often think of the choices my readers have had to make, and I thank God that I haven't been placed in many of those situations myself, although I certainly have had to face my share of tough and difficult decisions. But just a sampling of what my readers have had to deal with in their lives is enough to show how painful the dilemmas we all might end up facing can be:

- Your teenage son is a drug addict and you must face the prospect of kicking him out of the house.

- Your husband is killing himself with alcohol and you must somehow intervene.

- Your mother is in the last stages of terminal cancer, and she has asked you to help her "stop the pain."

- Your unmarried teenage daughter is pregnant.

- Your stepfather keeps making passes at you.

- You have started a business with a friend and discover that the friend is taking money from the till.

- Your newborn son needs a life-support system to keep him alive.

- Your parents have said they won't go to your wedding if you marry the man you love, who is of a different faith.

- You find out that your sister-in-law is having an affair, and you don't know if you should tell your brother.

All of these stories are real, and they are only a small portion of the ones my readers have told me about. In almost every case, though, and in all of the nine I've just listed, the person facing the dilemma overcame what seemed to be an insuperable problem and drew strength from it.

Like my readers, I believe we can all experience great pain and sorrow but still maintain a positive frame of mind. Everyone hungers for joy, and there is always something we can do to at least touch it, even at the worst moments in our lives.

There are very tangible things we can do every time we are confronted with tragedies or setbacks. We can take stock of ourselves and trust in the strength of our own inner resources. We can give ourselves the authority to be responsible for what happens to us, and to work our way out of it. We can be there for our loved ones in their time of need. We can come to a conscious decision to make our world better in many little ways, and we can see the quantitative change turn into a qualitative change. We can put grace and beauty into our lives.

What we don't want to be told is how we should live or feel. When we choose for ourselves, relying on our own consciences and our own knowledge of what is right, we almost invariably end up doing what we must in order to solve the problems facing us, to be decisive and get on with the business of living. As Eric Butterworth wisely reminds us, "We can always choose how we're going to react."

It is to a great many people that I owe the insights that help me through my own life, and most of all to the readers who have shared so much of themselves with me. And now, as I'm entering the second half of my existence, I feel that I in turn have a debt of gratitude to pay back. I hope that my writing about the choices I have made, and the choices I have seen the people around me make, will be as helpful to others as my readers have been to me.

Alexandra Stoddard

Alexandra Stoddard
Stonington Village,
Connecticut

We're faced with so many possibilities, so many options and alternatives. How can we look at a given situation objectively? Recognizing the role emotions play when we're faced with a serious choice, how can we always be sure to act intelligently and in our own best interest?

It's because of questions such as these that I love lecturing at colleges. The students are eager to make a difference in the world; they want to focus all their talents and passions on their goals, and they respond eagerly when I talk about the choices I've made and how they have helped me become the person I wished to be, professionally and personally. The most stimulating time in each talk is the question-and-answer period. I ask the young men and women what they want out of life, what they imagine themselves doing in five, ten, or twenty years. From their replies I have come to realize how difficult it is to make serious choices, and how many of them there really are. Yet I always come away from speaking to college students feeling happy and confident that many of them will affirm their passions by daring to take the leap of faith—by daring to express themselves.

The world seems increasingly complex, increasingly filled with ambiguities and unresolvable problems. The constant flux sets us whirling, and our options often seem complicated. All of us have the capability, however, to make solid choices that will work for us. Taking action is the key, but we can't use that key unless we know what doors we want to open. So how do we go about making our choices?

There are basic principles, tools to help us through, but

neither I nor anyone else can dictate the choices you will make. All I can do is encourage you to be brave and strong so that you *will* choose; not to do so may lead to the most awful loss of all: the loss of self, of opportunity, and, yes, joy. We've all, at times just hung back and done nothing and know how wrong we've been. We feel freest after we have made a hard decision on our own—and, after all, no one else will ever know enough about us to make the best choice *for* us.

The ability to make choices can be life-transforming. Nothing is preordained or predestined; it is our personal responsibility to choose for ourselves and live with our decisions. Simply doing so is a step toward freedom.

From as far back as I can remember, I've been fiercely independent. I first learned the importance of making choices when, at age seven, I began to tend my own garden. What my garden taught me is how inspiring it is to decide things for oneself. I pored over Burpee's seed catalogues, trying out different varieties of lettuce and zinnias; I had some great successes and an equal amount of duds. I tended not to dwell on the crops that never broke ground or the tomatoes that rotted green on the vine. What I most vividly remember were the rewards: the exhilarating sensation of running out the kitchen door in the early-morning light before breakfast, with dew still on the grass, dodging spiderwebs, running barefoot to see what was cooking in my precious garden. I was the youngest serious gardener in town, and I felt grown-up.

Claude Monet, whom I admire very much, loved flowers and good food just as I do. He collected garden catalogues and seed packets on his travels. He experimented, took risks, and had great success growing things no one else even dared to plant at Giverny. Judging by the abundance and splendor of his gardens, I'm certain that if something didn't work he'd rip it out and plant something else in its place. In the end, the real choice for Monet—and for me, and for all of us—was to create exactly the kind of garden he wanted, no matter what setbacks the process entailed.

Every man of courage is a man of his word.
—PIERRE CORNEILLE

TAKING ACTION

In a commencement address at Wellesley College, the writer Madeleine L'Engle challenged the students to dare to make difficult creative choices:

> We all have a marvelous combination of male and female within us, and part of maturing is learning to balance these two components so that they are the most fertile. It is only then that we are able to make creative choices and to understand that we do indeed have choices. . . . If we choose to remain ourselves, full of potential, then we can take whatever happens and redeem it by openness, courage, and willingness to move on. . . . When we believe in the impossible, it becomes possible, and we can do all kinds of extraordinary things.

She urged the graduates to make difficult decisions throughout their lives. Above all, she encouraged them to dare, to try, and always to choose.

Yet making choices requires taking risks and confronting our fears. What if we fail? What are the consequences? Decisions can be terrifying, since every time we choose something, we leap into the unknown. But regardless of risks, complexities, pain, or difficulties, there is everything to be said for wisely and courageously taking the plunge.

Whenever we make a choice, we must be willing to admit that we might make a mistake. It's hard, because it's something we will have to live with. Thus the most important thing is to think everything through before you decide; after that you just do it. Each time we hold back and don't choose, it's because we're hoping to not expose our shortcomings. When I first began to write, every new blank page in front of me was terrifying; although I knew what I wanted to express, I was afraid that any editor would pick my work apart. Yet I persevered, and now I have ten books behind me. But the key was that first step. Being passive and hesitant keeps us from developing our potential.

There are never absolutely right or wrong choices, and the ultimate answers to our questions don't always hit us like lightning. There is no one solution or path to take, no matter how long we ponder the questions. We will always live in a flowing stream of ambiguities and paradoxes, with the good and the bad, the gains and the losses. These dualistic tensions will *always* be there. Nothing is ever totally pleasant or painful, beautiful or ugly, lucky or unlucky.

A coward turns away, but a brave man's choice is danger.

—EURIPIDES

Courage conquers
all things.
—OVID

There are no *pure* choices; if there were, every decision would be easy. Life's mysteries aren't true-or-false questions.

Even when we know better, we like to fantasize that life will bear us painlessly toward our goals. It doesn't. Who ever fooled us into thinking we wouldn't get old? Who promised us that our lives would be spent in nothing less than perfect health? Who tricked us into thinking that money and power would bring us even a modicum of contentment?

Alan Watts tells us that "good without evil is like up without down." Likewise with our choices: each and every one of them isn't necessarily going to bring us closer to ultimate truth, success, and enlightenment. We try to be truthful, but once we admit that the choice we made didn't work, it's far easier to let go. We tried our best. As Emily Dickinson once said, "I dwell in possibilities." We do, too; what we choose to do, what we decide not to do, no matter what the outcome, will always be a daring act. Whenever I make a decision that turns out to be wrong, I then make the choice to back off. It doesn't matter if I made a mistake or if someone hurt me: when I make a decision I always feel an immediate sense of relief from knowing that I'm being honest with myself. I always get that wonderful sense of being back in control.

We often have to make a choice to get a monkey off our back or to walk away from an ugly situation. Certain choices we make inevitably leave us feeling empty and sad; but not to choose will make us feel worse.

We plow through a maze of alternatives, we weigh the

options, and we struggle to distinguish right from wrong. Not all our choices along the way will be momentous, but they will all be active. We may make a decision that is contradictory to what we actually want; but, on a deeper level, we know we must not follow our heart, but our conscience. Our heart is in love with someone who is married, for instance, so the right thing to do is choose *not* to act on our desires.

We are all victims at some point in our lives, when the choices we are faced with are beyond what a human being should bear. I once knew a young man who developed cancer of the eye, and the only way his doctors could hope to check the disease was to remove the eye. The young man couldn't bear to face the loss and refused to undergo the operation. But chemotherapy failed, the growth metastasized, and within a year the young man was dead. Tragedies don't go away by denial. Many choices makes us feel vulnerable and most involve fear, but all require *action.*

In 1977, when my mentor and boss, Eleanor McMillen Brown, retired at the age of eighty-eight as president of the design firm she founded in 1922, I quit. Looking back at it now, I realize that my decision wasn't exactly earthshaking, but at the time that's how it felt to me. I could never work for another boss. Even though I knew that I had to go, I became overwhelmed with apprehension. Leaving this old, established firm was risky to my career, to say nothing of my sense of identity. At Mrs. Brown's design firm I had a salary and clients. If I started my own company, I'd immediately have a payroll to meet and rent to pay. I had no capital and two young children. I'd be

No one can rob us of our free choice.
—EPICTETUS

Many people tell me they make big decisions all the time, but to make real choices is never painless. Whether to have fish or chicken for dinner is not a choice. I select one or the other based on my mood or the availability of fresh fish or whom I'm with. But choices are not preferences. Choices are serious and often have significant repercussions. Everyone suffers from the pain of making a decision; people who think they have no difficulty making choices are kidding themselves. To really choose, to really open up to greater possibilities, we must be willing to admit our vulnerability and take the better, harder road.

Self-deception, however, runs deep in human nature. If all choices are hard and require effort, no wonder so many people evade them. Even William James, the psychologist and philosopher, the great champion of pragmatism and free will, had difficulties making up his mind. When he was struggling to give up his lecturing at Harvard in his later years, one day he would write in his diary, "Resign," the next day, "Don't resign," the third day, "Resign."

This is the mark of a really admirable man: steadfastness in the face of trouble.
—LUDWIG VON BEETHOVEN

THE CHOICES TO MAKE

With each decision, we should be convinced that we're doing the best we can under the circumstances—best for ourselves, best for our family, best for our loved ones, and, possibly, best for society as well. A woman I know, a highly respected professor at a prestigious East Coast university, made a very difficult choice for which I admire her greatly. Her husband, a professor in another field, had been offered a post at a state university in the Midwest. Since the couple's last major professional decision had been to move to the East Coast city so that she could teach at the prestigious university, she felt it only fair that this major decision should revolve around *his* career; it was hard for her, but she felt that maintaining mutual respect in the marriage was more important to her than academic laurels. The results benefited everyone. Her husband is now the head of his department. The couple's children are thrilled to be living in a big house in the country instead of a cramped city apartment. The woman herself joined the midwestern university's faculty, which was very glad to have her. Under her direction, her new department has become a powerhouse in her field and rivals her old university in prestige. Her sacrifice, the choice that had been so hard to make, has not only made her life and her family's life better, but has literally made the world a better place.

There are only two kinds of choices available to us. First, the active: we make something happen and live with the consequences. Or we may choose to *not* make a choice; we weigh the facts, decide the price of change is too high and make the choice to live with things as they are. The second kind of choice, the more dangerous, it seems to me, is the postponement of choice. Procrastination results in apathy, discouragement, and depression. Whenever we turn our backs on what we *know* we need to do, we turn

> The strongest principle of growth lies in human choice.
> —GEORGE ELIOT

against our higher self. We forego the power to do something positive, to turn the situation around, or open new doors. At times we all want to think about problems tomorrow, but we lose sleep unnecessarily because we forfeit facing the truth. Our inability to confront the heart of the matter causes anxiety. Truth is *always* the right choice.

There is no magic in tomorrow; we can think things through rationally today. There are times, many times, when we just have to look truth in the face, bite the bullet, no matter how nasty or dirty or unpleasant the situation may be, and move on.

An amazing paradox is that it is really easier to be courageous than to be a coward. Once you get over the initial fear of plunging into the unknown, with all its dangers and snake traps, the mere fact that you dared to face a hard decision becomes your ally.

What we can teach ourselves to do is say yes and make a choice. We assess our situation with as clear a head as possible. I find it helpful to get out a piece of paper and draw a line down the center. On the top of the left-hand side I write "good," and on the top of the right-hand side I write "bad." I don't leave a space for "thinking about it tomorrow." This exercise has become a ritual to help me through specific problems. I see a choice before me—all I have to do is make it.

This habit of writing down what is and isn't going for you as you enter into a decision doesn't guarantee smooth sailing or sunny weather in the days ahead; it simply helps you to do the best you can right now.

Again, there are never perfect choices or ideal times to

The difficulty in life is the choice.
—GEORGE MOORE

make them. A friend confessed to me recently that she is torn in so many conflicting directions that she doesn't want to climb out of bed in the morning. We can't wait for perfect solutions; there aren't any. Perfection is a myth, something to strive toward but not be paralyzed by. It's a waste of time, talent, and creativity to feel that we must make the perfect decision—marry that perfect guy, write that perfect play, paint that masterpiece. What often happens is that we don't act at all. None of us had perfect childhoods; none of us have perfect spouses or children. None of us have perfect jobs, intellects, or judgment. Who among us never has never done anything dumb? What we do have is the ability to choose as wisely and rationally as possible with the cards we're dealt, with our personality quirks, our preconditioning, and our motivations factored in.

Nowhere in her writings or in her inspiring Wellesley address does Madeleine L'Engle ever discuss perfection; she talks about "creative realism" instead. By making choices, we learn to profit from our mistakes. Waiting for the perfect choice is to miss it all.

We have free will, but only once we face the reality of our options. We may not have the greatest job, but we have chosen a certain offer as the best of all the opportunities available to us. Or the work we're doing may not be what we want for the rest of our lives, but it pays the rent. Many of us go through coasting periods in our lives. But when we choose to cope, we are able to maintain our independence; we come to look pragmatically at our less-than-perfect but real circumstances. Realism, never perfection, is the key to wise choice-making.

> It is better that joy should be spread over all the day in the form of strength than that it should be concentrated into ecstasies....
>
> —RALPH WALDO EMERSON

Yet all our choices take a particular time frame into account—although, granted, timing isn't quite an exact science. We can choose to have babies when we're young; when we're fifty, we have no choice. If we don't act at the right time, we miss the opportunity. But most important: not choosing is never a good solution. It becomes a habit, a pattern. The person who passively sits back, who waits and sees, will never feel too terrific about life because there will never be much electricity, satisfaction, or fulfillment in it. Nothing works out when nothing is going on. There's always something both wise and brave about getting back on the horse after you've fallen off.

Courage is the best attitude with which to approach choices because it becomes a tool, our means to greater self-expression and freedom. The most awful sensation imaginable is to be stuck between two opposite poles, in the middle of a cacophonous shouting match of emotions. You feel the powerful storm pulling at you in all directions, switching winds that catch you off guard. You feel torn apart. Yet these conflicts can be resolved by thinking things through and then choosing, even if later on it becomes obvious that the decision isn't working out. When we make a plan, we gain a feeling of being intensely alive. We become more aware of our *self*, of our own deliberations, which is exhilarating. Again, the key thing is that you *must* take action. And when you believe in something, your choices will bear witness to that. Always listen to the questions stirring up inside you, and never seek absolute answers from others.

It's true that we tend to have difficulties admitting

when something isn't right for us. We feel a sense of guilt and failure when, for instance, we back out of something we've said yes to—voices from our childhood taunt us with the words "perseverance" and "stick-to-itiveness" (a favorite of my mother's). But we must always be brave, even when being brave means quitting. A child decides on a college, enrolls, and, once there, hates it for some good reason and leaves. You start a new job but your boss is an alcoholic, so you resign. In a dying marriage, for example, who but the husband and wife really knows the facts? Let's go back to the two kinds of choices. You can say that you loathe your husband, are miserable, and choose to leave him. Or you can continue to live with him because of your vows, your children, a glimmer of hope that things might get better. Or you can sit back and endure untold misery as a martyr, a hopeless victim. You feel stuck forever. Trapped. Your whole life is doomed.

But just because we made a mistake doesn't mean we can't correct it. Admitting something isn't right for you requires a great deal of wisdom, but a wisdom we can all make ours now.

Let's say the sixteen-year-old girl who lives down the street gets pregnant. She *has* to make a choice. She can try to get the boy to marry her and then have the baby. She can remain single, raising it herself or giving it up for adoption. She can make the anguishing choice to get an abortion. Or she can do nothing and think about it later. Whatever she decides, her options diminish the longer she procrastinates. The girl has an easier time choosing than most of us do, in many ways, because she has a built-in

Your outlook on life is a conscious choice.
—SUSAN MURRAY YOUNG

to take the necessary chances to make it work. When I look back on the proudest moments in my life, I realize how many risks they involved. As a junior nationally ranked tennis player, I didn't win all my matches, not by a long shot, but I kept playing. Before I knew it, my game improved; I began to win more and more matches. The choice I made was to give my all to tennis for a certain period of time. It was a vital experience for me.

I learned as a teenager that I'd rather be creamed off the court by a superior player than win a match that was patty-cake and boring, all lobs and drop shots. That mentality remains with me today. I chose tough competition then, and I came across opponents who made me look like a duffer, but at least I was beaten by players of skill and discipline who went on to win international titles. When Billie Jean King defeated me in straight sets at the Junior Nationals in Pennsylvania, my mother told everyone that the match was "close." The truth was that I was clearly outmatched, but I felt better losing to Billie Jean than winning any number of weekend tennis club games.

Fear of failure is a huge barrier to living a full, creative, heroic life. Choosing will always provide opportunities. We learn to trust our ability to make decisions, and our greatest lessons come from the ones that prove to be wrong. Taking risks is our chance to find out what works for us, what we can do well. We will never lose if we define and redefine ourselves after each failure. We learn to choose what we want and not to worry about the rest. If we're the best we can be, we learn to respect what we *can* become in the future.

As adults, we're responsible for our own behavior. When we hold ourselves personally accountable for what we do, we find ourselves unable to shrug blame off on anyone else. If the larger percentage of our choices is right for us, if they ring true to our conscience, we will become known for the integrity of what we choose to do and choose not to do. Take a stand. Vote for the best candidate. Be accountable. Be reliable. Our authenticity and integrity are not mirrored by our appearance, power, or wealth; who we are is ultimately reflected in the honesty of our choices. When we make choices that we believe in, we're making an effort to follow the truth as we see and experience it. This in and of itself is a liberating path.

How do we set our limits? How can we shape and form our life so we're productive as well as fulfilled? There are just so many hours in the day. We're stretched. We can't do it all any more than we can win them all; we must make choices. Only a keen sense of what we must do will give order to our life and allow us to develop the patterns, rhythms, and rituals that we can depend and rely on. Only our solid choices will bring us contentment and peace amid the anxiety and commotion that surround us. Yet how do we handle the guilt and resentment we'll encounter when we try to do that which lets us feel committed, satisfied, and fulfilled?

Others will always try to judge and criticize you when you think and act independently. When you accept that as inevitable, you will be able to break free and make your *own* choices. People will disagree and argue with you, attack, fight, undermine, manipulate, accuse, and try to upset

Speak the affirmative; emphasize your choice by utter ignoring of all that you reject.

—RALPH WALDO EMERSON

you if your choices don't square with what *they* want. When you assert your will rather than theirs, you'll experience friction. The choices you make *will* disappoint some, but you'll make it up to those you care deeply for by living—and loving—honestly, on your own terms and in your own way.

A woman I once met in Colorado is one of the best examples of such a person. A first-rate organizer and administrator, she had been on the board of several large charities in her state, and everyone who worked with her knew that her contributions were invaluable. At one point, while she was running a cancer fund-raiser, she met a child who was dying of the disease. Suddenly she realized that working with dying children was what she most wanted to do—it was very literally her calling. As her focus changed she began spending less and less time with other charities, and of course her colleagues were disappointed. Some even began to resent her. But she knew that her work with the children was far more important, and she took her ex-colleagues' reaction in stride. She now works exclusively with dying children, and her love and commitment have touched hundreds of lives. By remaining true to her inner self, her calling, she has profoundly changed the world around her.

You're the one who has to make your own decisions because you're the only one who can figure out what you have to do. You're the one who lives with the consequences of your choices. Choose *not* to be under the spell of controlling personalities—not a mother, a father, a husband, a wife, a child, a friend, a teacher, a spiritual leader, a neighbor, a boss, a partner, or a committee member. Ultimately, your

The will is that by which the mind chooses anything.
—JONATHAN EDWARDS

choices are what separate you from everyone else. They are the only road to becoming truly independent.

Søren Kierkegaard, the Danish philosopher and theologian, tells us, "Truth exists only as the individual himself produces it in action." Choose—it is the only way.

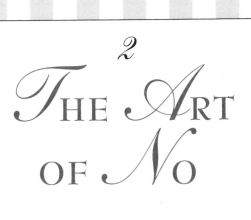

2

The Art of No

> "The most common despair is to be in despair of not choosing, or willing, to be oneself; but…the deepest form of despair is to choose to be another than oneself."
>
> —SØREN KIERKEGAARD

SAYING NO

No is an essential art; it is disciplining, restraining, guiding; it is the linchpin of an ordered, balanced, healthy, full life. No is not an end in itself, but a way of dealing with the contradictions, the flux that is constantly around us. It is complex and subtle, and calls for wisdom to be used well. No is your constant companion, the way to keep you on your own path.

Both as a technique and an art, no lies at the heart of an effective personality. Given the spectrum of choices that face us, it is a necessity. Once we embrace it as a means to take care of our own needs, we can become more genuinely who we are. We have to look at it as a living, real, vital process that goes on throughout our lives. Once properly understood, no becomes a tool, a way to regulate and maintain your life, face up to your obligations as well as your needs, accept your limitations, and pay close attention to your conscience. No is a way of governing your time, energy, and resources so you can see your *self* clearly in relationship to the rest of the world.

Once you have decided what you wish to do, what you believe is the *right* thing under the circumstances, no allows you to weed out what is redundant, excessive, inappropriate, or conflicting. By liberating you to go forward confident that you're doing what is right, no becomes a rudder that keeps you from randomly drifting with the currents.

No is the best way to keep on path, to sort through the often contradictory signals we receive whenever we try to come closer to the truth. It restrains us, giving our life necessary structure, defining, honing, and focusing on who we are and what out potential is. It is a way to keep us from excess or drifting in a direction that is not of *our* own choosing. Whenever we enjoy too much of a good thing, we feel it. I love to have a glass of good wine with dinner, but *not* with breakfast. No sets down rules for your lifestyle the way grammar does for good prose.

The current healthy trend toward a more realistic, wholesome lifestyle requires careful checks and balances. We have to invent ways of adjusting to the swirling world around us, and we do this by staying calm at our center. Not only do we have to choose what's important—our family, our home, privacy, good health, strong political and spiritual leaders—but we must also have a positive attitude about life.

We alone have to figure out how to accomplish our

... While every pleasure is in itself good, not all pleasures are to be chosen.

—EPICURUS

goals. We must learn to better appreciate and value what we *already* have. Realistically, all we can be sure of is that we will choose to make the most of our time, being and doing according to the principles that we believe are right.

The art of no helps you to carry on, pursuing a chosen course, trying to do what's best, regardless of the roadblocks and detours. I remember saying no to an important decorating job when my daughter Brooke was a senior in high school. What we shared at the kitchen table that year *far* outweighed what I would have gained from one more decorating job. A year later I would have embraced the opportunity, but all possibilities are bound by constraints of time. No one waits for you, especially not your children. They grow up whether you're there to be with them or not.

There are subtle ways we can redirect ourselves when we've temporarily lost our way; we take care of what's really important at the moment, letting go of what matters less. No is never a rigid black-or-white decision, but more like a clear stream flowing from one thing to another with no beginnings or endings. The art of no provides ease and grace, allowing us enough room to invite spontaneity, even serendipity, into our lives—if we give it a chance. As the great Chinese philosopher Lao-tzu said so beautifully twenty-five centuries ago in the *Tao-te-ching:* "The way to do is to be." This has been my favorite maxim for a long time. If we ease up a bit, back off a little, pace ourselves, catch our breath, free up a frenzied schedule, we'll find joy in *being.* The simplest of things, like a bird singing outside our window, will not go unappreciated. So to be is to live in concert with the moment. No provides time and space to live in harmony with the rhythms of the day.

To be at home for dinner with the family tonight means saying no to working late, or to the professional reception or dinner party. *Being* at home with your family—relaxed, attentive, participating—is a real opportunity. Family time is for you to choose. When the children are grown, living somewhere else, on their own, your schedule will be free— you can incorporate many more professional receptions and dinner parties in your calendar. But to lose sight of the importance of *being* there when your family is in the nest means a permanent loss to both you and your children.

To say no to an invitation because you'd already planned a delicious evening in front of the fire with your family might not move the mercury above the 98.6 mark. But it could. Sure, you feel a tug because you have to give up a party you'd really like to go to. You say no, but feel a flush of indecision. You're frustrated because you'll miss seeing your college roommate from Chicago. It's not the end of the world. There will be another time. You stick to your plan and things will work out.

Nothing materializes without a program. If we don't make arrangements to be together with our family regularly, we will find the years slipping by. Saying no to a friend's party in order to be with your family shouldn't present a dilemma. The essence of no is to have priorities and keep them in order.

When the girls were teenagers, Peter and I made a rule that we'd stay home Friday and Saturday nights—supervising curfews, inviting their friends to spend the night if they didn't feel up to driving home. We never suffered from indecision about whether we should or shouldn't be

Men must be decided on what they will not do, and then they are able to act with vigor in what they ought to do.

—MENCIUS

there; being at home automatically eliminated the possibility of being anywhere else. The art of no is a bit easier when you remember that you can be only *one* place at a time. We put everything else on the back burner during those formative years. Looking back, I can't imagine having chosen to be anywhere else. It was during those peaceful weekends that we learned the calming effects of no as an art.

CONSCIENCE AND COMMITMENTS

Throughout our lives we are subject to our conscience, to the guiding inner voice. So what our conscience tells us *not* to do is as important as our deliberate choices to act. No has a negative ring to many, but if we don't look at it clearly and *use* it, we will lose the opportunity to discipline ourselves, to manage our own affairs. The reason each of us has to develop no into an art is because once we understand our own limits—once we focus on what is right and eliminate what is *not* right—we'll have to learn to politely turn others down. People who are embarrassed to reject someone else's suggestions, who are bullied or bully themselves into saying yes, suffer unnecessarily. The pressure others put on you, manipulating you into feeling you *should* or *ought to* do something, is completely external, and it has no power over you unless you allow it. Even greater is the pressure we put on ourselves. Sometimes the ghosts from our past—parents, teachers, spiritual leaders, mentors, friends—haunt us. We have internalized what we *think* are their expectations for us. This only leads to guilt, lack of clarity, and loss of self. If something isn't right for you, there's no reason to do it.

Constantly giving in to other people's demands may give you an air of selflessness, but in effect it is an abdication of personal responsibility. Remember you said yes to this real or imagined *demand*. Now you own it; it is your choice.

No is real. It helps you to determine what's important to you and puts a distance between you and the things that aren't right for you. It eliminates wasting *your* time; it's telling the truth. You move away from unrealistic expectations and the pressure of others on you. Once you embrace the art of no, you can only move in the direction of what *you* choose to do. You can responsibly meet your obligations and at the same time make room to enjoy idle moments of stargazing or putting up your feet in your own backyard (a high priority with me).

You need not be a yesaholic unless you choose to be. You're not under any obligation to accept any request, regardless of how tempting it may seem. As they say, just because you can doesn't mean you should. You can examine the choice closely each time. You think: "Is this me?" "This is *not* what I choose to do." "This is not what I have in mind." "This is not right for me."

No saves you from the dangerous myth that you're indispensable. Nobody has ever succeeded in being all things to all people. The reason no is so difficult at first is that many of the demands made on us appear as though they are *our* responsibility. Don't accept anything as your obli-

Examine each opinion: if it seems true, embrace it; if false, grid up thy mind to withstand it.

—LUCRETIUS

gation until you're willing to embrace it as your commitment. The onus is not on you until you say yes. We were raised to feel that we should give back what we can; we feel we owe it to a world that has given us so much. But who ever said we're obligated to take care of everything?

Many people don't know what they want to do with their lives, and therefore they are particularly vulnerable to reacting passively to well-meaning people and worthy causes. Whenever you're not guided by your own compass, you will drift around constantly, not necessarily getting anywhere worthwhile or meaningful.

Eventually you'll discover that it's cowardly to give in to what others ask of you rather than doing what you know is right for you. Others shouldn't make you feel guilty about it.

There will always be those who'd like to boss us around, and whenever we're under the thumb of controlling individuals we experience constant pressure, we harbor resentment, we feel manipulated. I've seen this syndrome in many marriages, especially when the husband is the sole breadwinner. He feels he can be demanding because he's footing the bills. This controlling attitude is cruel and heartbreaking. I was working with a client one afternoon and we were running late. We hadn't stopped for lunch—something I try never to do—and when Carol called her husband, Don, to ask him if she could meet him at the theater instead of at his office that evening, he said no; he insisted that she pick up the tickets and meet him in front of his office at five, as scheduled. Carol came away from the telephone in tears. "I have to leave immediately," she said. "I'm sorry." I felt empathy for her, but her be-

Man's task is simple: he should cease letting his "existence" be a thoughtless accident.

—FRIEDRICH NIETZSCHE

BEING A MARTYR

We learn to say no to ourselves all the time. It's character-building; we feel good when we deny ourselves. Whenever we have to deny someone else their wishes, however, we begin to feel anxious and guilty. We immediately ask ourselves if we do enough for others in general; we wonder whether, in fact, we might just be hopelessly selfish. Why do we feel so threatened when someone invites us to join them in a good cause? Why is it so difficult to turn something down even when we know we don't have the resources, the time, or the commitment to live up to it? Where do we draw the line?

The 1980s showed us the exhilaration syndrome; people became stimulus junkies, breathless, stressed, burned out. The hyperactivity of the 1980s was in large part material; spurred on by one of the biggest consumer binges in history, by the millions we sacrificed everything to earn or borrow our way into the unprecedented wealth we saw everywhere around us—we made ourselves martyrs to money. Now, seeking a balance, many of us are choosing to simplify our lives. This is not a cop-out. None of our lives, by definition, is simple. It's far more difficult to artfully use no as a discipline than to give in and go along with the crowd.

Yet although the 1980s bubble has burst, the same kind of frenetic activity—and its side effects—still remains with

...the decision in favor of his integrity may be held to be morally superior to that in favor of his life.

—ERICH FROMM

us, even if in other forms. Whether it's working for five charities or staying up three straight days trading junk bonds, it's still excess. Whenever you take on the problems of the world, you verge on being a martyr. There are few saints among us, and fewer still who take on excessive amounts of work without bragging about it. "Oh, I made five hundred sandwiches for the church fair." "I stayed up until three-thirty A.M. writing letters requesting donations for the school gym." "I spent the weekend making robes for the church choir." All this complaining is a form of self-flattery. A do-gooder doing good, with little time left for sleep or leisure. Who expects you to stay up half the night? Who appreciates the sacrifice of your weekend to fulfill your self-imposed obligations? If you crave sympathy for all your labors, by definition you're seeking validation from the outside. Doing worthwhile things for others should not wreck your emotional balance; it should be fun.

Whenever we take on something that becomes a burden rather than a blessing, we revert to childhood behavior: complaining, seeking pity, feeling sorry for ourselves. But the true spirit of giving springs naturally from within and is executed with enthusiasm, energy, and great satisfaction. It seems odd to accept an obligation and then to moan and groan while carrying it out. When we enjoy what we're doing, when we feel useful and content, we rarely need to brag about it because the fun and pleasure is in the act itself.

Consider what your motives are when you accept responsibilities that make you feel frantic and frenzied. We can't blame others for inviting us to join a worthy cause. Whose choice is it to accept?

Almost everything is a combination of good and bad. We must make choices. We must give up some good to avoid the bad, and accept some bad to retain the good.... The fact is that choice is the highest level of human functioning.

—AARON STERN

To dabble in volunteering randomly, flitting from one project to another, might initially seem easier than to take a stand and do things that come together to express something personal. You rationalize that you feel good working on behalf of others. It's your duty; it keeps you busy; you're lonely.

The only certainty about doing things for others is that every yes inevitably subjects you to more demands. The saying that if you give an inch they'll take a mile sounds cynical, but it's true. No one ever asks you to give *less* the next time; *more* is just the accepted pattern. It is for this reason that we should all be as thoughtful and careful about saying yes as we can.

MAINTAINING A BALANCE

To decline an invitation gracefully, excusing yourself without offending anyone or feeling like a wretched person, is a tricky thing. No matter how artful your dodge may be, someone else's urging often borders on being a command. Maintaining a necessary balance is arduous, something we struggle with throughout our lives.

Having a plan and sticking to it is next to impossible, given the likelihood of the interruptions—good and bad— that inevitably crop up in our lives. But not to have an agenda, not to fill up your own dance card, is no solution. We must actively decide what we wish to do, make a plan, and get going. But we can't unthinkingly fill up our calendar, busying ourselves with a surfeit of obligations, merely getting through events, never leaving ourselves enough space to regroup. We must focus on the direction *we* choose our life to take. Only when you figure this out can you avoid feeling guilty about editing out the non-essentials. When we look at the big picture and plan ahead, we see more clearly who we are, our priorities become clearer, and we can honestly face our limitations.

No is not negative; it actively leads to the positive. My own struggle to accept certain restrictions on my time, energy, and money have helped me to reach my goals. I'm often asked how I have time to do everything. My answer is clear. It is what I *don't* do that gives me the freedom to do what I wish.

So no is a pattern of choices; the key is to establish your own objectives so you won't veer off course. By not doing hundreds of little things you don't need to do, you're free to pursue your work, spend time with a child or spouse, relax in a hammock, or read a good book. Look ahead. Keep your real commitments in mind when you exercise no. The feeling that your life is flowing in the direction of your choices helps keep you on course. If we stay true to our chosen lifestyle, exercising no, we'll find ourselves treading less water than we might have in the past.

Many of us have trouble balancing everything. When I look at what we're doing day to day, I can see why. Many of us are raising children, working, taking care of a home, keeping in touch with friends and family, doing church work. Equally important, we are also attempting to deepen our psychological lives; we're struggling to figure out what

For what I will, I will, and there an end.
—WILLIAM SHAKESPEARE

everything means to us, trying to understand more about ourselves, about how we can live more fully. And thus, for a series of complex reasons, many of us have become time-bankrupt. We've given more away than we have.

In *Living Beautifully Together*, I suggested we take ten percent of our waking time for ourselves. Women with small children are the ones who find this next to impossible, but they are the ones who need it most. Many of us are doing too much, and the consequences are serious because it can become a chronically stressful condition in which we lose all sense of perspective. When I was raising my children, no matter how exhausted I was or how late I had stayed up the night before, I set my alarm for five o'clock each weekday morning. I got up, made myself some coffee, went into the living room to my writing table, and read or wrote. This was the only time when I wouldn't be interrupted. The ritual usually provided two pure, quiet hours to work before the real day began. This daily pattern allowed me to think things through in peace each morning, and it regularly renewed my spirit.

The peaceful, private time before the sun rose was my own. I was free. I could daydream or write. I lit candles and wrote letters. I read inspirational books. Was I tired? Yes! Did I have black circles under my eyes? Yes! But it was worthwhile. It was personal. No one knew what I was doing; no one was asking me to do it. I was committed to writing no matter how full the rest of my life became. I had to say no to sleeping through the alarm. After several months, this early-morning spa for the soul became a compulsive passion. In retrospect, I realize it was from it that

A gilded no is more satisfactory than a harsh yes.

—BALTASAR GRACIÁN

I developed my ten percent theory. My ten hours every week, Monday through Friday, was a little more than ten percent of my waking hours.

During that stressful, intensely busy period in my life—raising Alexandra and Brooke, working a high-powered job at Mrs. Brown's design firm, and teaching myself how to write—I caught flu a lot. I was once home sick in bed on a day my mother and I had planned to have lunch together. She came over to see me. When she walked into my bedroom and caught me writing, my papers scattered all over the bedcovers, she reprimanded me: "Darling, don't work. You're sick. Take some time off." I paid no attention to her advice. As soon as she left, I continued working on an article about color schemes, which fascinated me and took my mind off my aches and pains; the article ended up being excerpted in *Reader's Digest*.

Like most mothers—though they aren't always right—my mother was well meaning. Since I was ill, she felt I should rest my brain as well as my body. But my mind was happy to get some exercise. I loved what I was doing, and I was doing it for myself. Just because your body has been attacked by a virus doesn't mean you can't think and create.

Self-expression is one of the most urgent human needs. Though their health was failing, Monet, van Gogh, and Renoir all painted until the very end. No one else can know what is best for us. We can be advised, we can listen, but ultimately we must choose for ourselves. While my mother was concerned with my physical health, I instinctively attended to the mind and spirit.

What a commentary on civilization, when being alone is considered suspect; when one has to apologize for it, make excuses, hide the fact that one practices it—like a secret vice.

—ANNE MORROW LINDBERGH

There's small choice
in rotten apples.
—WILLIAM SHAKESPEARE

THE TIME FOR NO

I've spent these last thirty years watching how people politely or not so politely put pressure on others. Often without knowing it, but nevertheless with great effectiveness,
someone always wants to run our lives. But a book doesn't
get written, a canvas doesn't get painted, a mountain
doesn't get climbed, without our taking the time to do it.
We can't expect anyone else to understand what we really
may be trying to express in our lives and work. Think of
the terrible things contemporary critics said of the Im-
pressionists. Monet went beyond representational painting—he was trying to convey mood, light, and atmosphere.
Judging from the current Monet mania, he succeeded in
stirring *us*, a hundred years later, with his unique vision.

We don't have to be literally engaged in doing something else in order to say no. The freedom and benefits of
saying no should have nothing to do with how busy we are.
It is instead largely a state of mind that frees us from the
habit of stuffing our schedules with everything that comes
our way, everything under the sun, as though quantity will
bring us quality of life. Who ever feels really terrific when
they overeat? Isn't overdoing just as depressing?

Being able to skillfully exercise no implies having the
inner resources to withdraw a bit from the world. When
Peter and I bought our house in Connecticut, we thought
we would go there to write. However, something quite

different occurred during the first two years. We were naturally drawn by nesting instinct to fix up the house. After painting all day, we wanted to sit, look out over the water, experience the sunset, and share a moment's peace. We now look back, realizing how impossible it would have been to enjoy writing in a dingy, depressing dump. We had to create an environment that was both stimulating and serene and that would inspire our best work. We never woke up deliberately saying we wouldn't write, but somehow that just evolved into a pattern, and lasted until our house was fully restored. While the public wasn't invited into Monet's walled garden during his lifetime, he was sharing it through his art. I believe his garden was an essential choice in order for him to express his own vision. In the same way, we often have to do one thing to prepare for something else. This is why no is such a necessity. We eventually learn to reject other people's proposals in favor of our own (except, of course, when the fit is right).

Peter and I were content to go to our retreat, quietly, privately fixing it up, being alone together. We didn't divulge to anyone what our plans were; we just enjoyed what we were creating for ourselves—an escape from the pressures, dangers, and stresses of our life in the city. For several months, we didn't tell more than two or three people that we'd even bought the house. We made our plans to go whenever we were free of our work commitments, saying no to everything that would interfere with our time together. Those two quiet years of escape were revitalizing. Our children were grown up, our parents dead. We had no duties to perform. We were under no one's thumb. The time fixing up our old house was largely free from stress.

The moments of freedom, they can't be given to you. You have to take them.

—ROBERT FROST

that is interfering with what you truly want to do?

The larger portion of our interests and responsibilities is invariably of our own choosing. When we have children, for example, we can never accurately predict when our time and attention will really be needed. The obligations we willingly take on become all-consuming at certain stages, requiring flexibility and a sense of humor. When our responsibilities are assumed by choice, we must always be there fully when a legitimate need arises; but when the crisis is resolved, we should be able to return to our own plans again. It is vitally important to maintain a part of us that is not directly connected to spouse, child, job, or charity. If you're sure about what you want to express, about that secret part of you, you're on the right track. If you're not, it's time to start thinking hard.

Ideally we should recognize what we value out of the possibilities open to us. We have the ability to set our own limits. We affirm where we are in our quest, what we're attempting to do, and by understanding no as an art we allow ourselves the space for solitude, reflection, and private work. Once we have accepted and understood our limits, we can begin to embrace no as preventive medicine.

No doesn't have to be wrenching. You're going to say no anyway; what makes the difference is how to do it gracefully, with as much diplomacy as possible. No makes you sensitive to the feelings of others; at the same time, it makes you more aware of your own feelings. The person you reject need not be hurt. If someone asks you to do something that's not right for you at the time, you can thank them for thinking of you, but explain your circumstances. The person asking something of you is experienc-

> Personality can never develop unless the individual chooses his own way, consciously and with moral deliberation.
>
> —CARL JUNG

ing life differently; no helps us feel comfortable with the wealth of differences between us, no matter how shared our basic values may be. What is right for one person at a particular time could be poison for another.

When you say no, express it unambiguously. Never say maybe. Many possibilities arise at different stages in our lives, but when we know something is wrong, we have to reverse our yes and turn it into no. Saying maybe confuses and brings no relief. Maybe is unfinished business. No is crisp, clear, clean, and final; it is the bottom line.

Actively say no. When you say good-bye to the weeds you didn't plant, you make room for flowers of your choice. Get in the habit of acting rather than reacting. Move with greater harmony and effectiveness by disciplining yourself rather than feeling constant and indiscriminate responsibility toward others.

We can be dedicated and useful without losing our sense of pleasure in what we're doing. When something fits us in mind, body, and spirit, when we are equipped for it psychologically, have the intelligence and the talent to carry it out, we can work happily and with a sense of fulfillment. Hemingway wrote passionately; absorbed in a trancelike state, he became one with what he was doing. That is why his words are alive. No, as art, saves you from racing around breathless and in the wrong gear. When is the last time you were so engrossed in something deeply your own that you lost track of time?

At times, the voices of others register louder than our own inner voice. The greater their pressure, the more discipline no requires. Because it's much easier to get yourself into something than to get out of it, calmly let your intui-

Either control your own destiny, or someone else will.
—JOHN F. WELCH, JR.

61

tion guide you. Whenever you agree to do something because you feel sorry for someone, or out of guilt, you'll end up paying too great a price. Remember that no is subtle. It can be exercised so gracefully that everyone gains and no one feels guilt. But the most important thing to keep in mind is that no is your greatest treasure; it's your bulwark against the unwelcome and the inappropriate. No brings immediate relief.

Just because you can doesn't necessarily mean you should.

—CARL BRANDT

THE ESSENCE OF NO

Whatever you take on affects your subconscious. I've never been much good at anything unless I give myself to it one hundred percent. If we don't give our best, we'll let down the people who asked for our help, and in fact they'll be the first to criticize us when we start to give less. Yes always means going an extra mile. But how many of us can continue to go the extra mile for long without becoming exhausted?

Whenever you have any doubt about how appropriate a given responsibility is for you, ask yourself if someone else could do the same task in order to free you for something that perhaps only you can do. It really doesn't matter *who* does the job as long as it gets done. Learn to delegate, to recommend others. If you can't give your all, say so openly and honestly.

You're good at budgeting your household purchases—food, home maintenance, insurance, clothes, and travel.

You plan for your children's education as well as for your retirement. But often the most enormously capable budgeter and planner has blind spots when it comes to understanding the limits of a twenty-four-hour day. The fact is that there's no guarantee that we'll always be blessed with radiant health and vibrant energy. There will be times when we're temporarily knocked out of the race. Likewise, there will always be things we wish we could do and that sound like fun. The menu of attractive options increases the more we move around, the more people we meet, the more we say yes. Be forewarned.

We have to continually make up new rules in the face of unexpected conflicts. The art of no requires paying attention to the smallest details while thinking of the big picture, because when we pay attention and are aware, we never need to feel trapped or pessimistic. No is our constant companion, our guardian against steering the wrong, often dangerous course. And when we do become derailed, we can instantly exercise no and concentrate on getting back on track. No protects constantly and absolutely.

What are some limits you want to establish for yourself in the near future? What are some of the nos you believe are best for you, taking into consideration the immediate needs of your spouse, your children, your job, your partner, and yourself? I recently learned from a client that he turned down an opportunity for a high-paying job because he didn't feel it was the right time to relocate his family. A forty-year-old newly married woman I know chose to give up for the time being a stressful career in investment banking in order to try to start a family. A sacrifice isn't necessarily cause for disappointment. Karen found nesting

Sometimes it is a good choice not to choose at all.
—MICHEL DE MONTAIGNE

very satisfying. If we treat it reverently, no will fan out in all directions, helping us live our own life.

No, properly understood, opens us up to a far deeper optimism and sense of well-being. Until we find time for developing our no skills, we can become unglued by a phone call, unexpected bills, sudden knocks on the door, or a demand from a loved one or boss. No gives us time out, a break, time to carry on with our own chosen plans. But with every freedom also comes the enormous burden of responsibility. As with every choice, when we use no, we must consider how it will affect others.

When elevated, sustained, and maintained, no is the essence of selflessness. The individual who has mastered the art is ready to live fully, understanding and accepting the inevitability of setbacks, but enthusiastically engaging in a series of choices that add up to the nearest we'll ever come to being perfect.

The imitator dooms himself to hopeless mediocrity.

—RALPH WALDO EMERSON

3

BITING THE BULLET

"The artful denial of a problem will not
produce conviction; on the contrary, a wider
and higher consciousness is required to give
us the certainty and clarity we need."

—CARL JUNG

TIMES OF CRISIS

Sooner or later, each of us comes across situations in which
we have to bite the bullet. When we're presented with
tragedy, we have to realize that the damage has *already*
been done. When we confront something deadly serious,
we give up our rationalizations, our illusions, our unrealistic dreams, and we face the way things really are.

For whatever reason, regardless of where the fault lies,
there will be times when you have to admit you're in crisis.
The cause could be a tragic death, an illness, an accident,
the loss of a job, rape, burglary, a fire, a flood, a partner
who cheats on you, anything.

Regardless of how complex the facts are, no matter
how seemingly insurmountable the difficulties, you have to

actually a relief—physically, mentally, and spiritually. Problems never mysteriously go away, and when they're neglected they multiply.

When we come to a decision, we are actually getting back on our path. In many cases, we find a negative turning into a positive. We're no longer stuck. We take action to fix something that doesn't work. We choose to change things around; the tools are in our hands. Just attacking the situation empowers us.

When we see and face an awkward problem directly, then we're in a position to *do* what has to be done rather than merely worrying about it. When we try to do what must be done, appreciating the resources we have, refusing to dwell on what has just been taken away from us, we can get on with rebuilding our lives, and will be better off because of the experience.

Think positively about cutting your losses, not about how awful your situation may be. A woman I know, a former model, developed breast cancer that resulted in a double mastectomy. By having the operation immediately, she was able to arrest the cancer. She is one of the lucky survivors. How does Gail feel about losing her breasts? How would any woman feel? Did she have a choice? She could have been a coward, feeling sorry for herself, procrastinating until her cancer metastasized. She chose life over death. With the help of family, friends, and therapy, Gail is now living fully, helping to inspire and encourage other women who are facing this painful operation. As a result of her strength, Gail has become a powerful role model and is saving women's lives every day. We all must learn the hard way that we are not alone. Our suffering is

Only through the struggle of choosing can we become the good soil.

—REV. SPENCER M. RICE

individual, but the strength we draw from it has universal effects.

I remember with great sadness being at my father's bedside one Christmas morning when he was about to have his right leg amputated below the knee. The last words he said as he dozed off under the anesthetic were, "I don't want to wake up if they take off my leg, dear." My father knew that he was having his leg amputated—that was the reason he was in the hospital. But to his mind, he was dying; without his leg, he would no longer be alive, he would no longer be whole. The stump had to be amputated a second time, months later, this time *above* the knee. The situation was too much for him. His spirit broke, and his remaining years were spent in misery. In a sense, he chose to die prematurely; he smoked himself to a fatal heart attack. Who knows? Maybe my father could be alive today if he had given up smoking before it was too late. Reform would be a whole lot easier if we could visualize the long-term consequences of our behavior, but we are too quick to think that these dreadful things happen to our neighbors rather than to ourselves.

Some brave souls, however, lift us up to a higher level because of the sheer strength of their self-awareness. There are a lot of gutsy men and women who can become our teachers and mentors, people we look up to who have had to face and surmount almost overwhelming tragedies.

When we're young, we feel not only indestructible, but omnipotent. We're daredevils on the fast track, burning the candle at both ends, trying to get away with murder. We drink and drive. We experiment with sex and drugs. By the time we've matured, however, we've experienced so

Where there is no choice, we do well to make no difficulty.
—GEORGE MACDONALD

69

much sadness that we live with a dull sense of discourage-ment, an awareness of war, illness, and death. We've seen too much: accidents, fires, robberies, frauds, suicides, rapes, murders, government mismanagement, environmen-tal decay, spiritual debilitation. Healthy optimists or not, eventually we all become disillusioned.

In a few, rare situations, anger is the right way to respond, but make the decision to react a conscious choice.

—LYNDA POWELL

History in this sense is our tutor. There is no period in recorded time, not even a moment, that has been entirely free from danger, illness, or despair. There is bad news out there every day. It enters our bedrooms, our living rooms, the places where our children are. Even when our own life is going well, we fret about the deteriorating quality of life all over the globe. Aware of how interconnected we are, all of us feel hopeless about our personal inability to make a real difference. The massive, entrenched battle lines we see everywhere mystify and discourage us.

Yet despite this, there *is* room for an optimistic attitude. If we didn't somehow counterbalance the bad news in the papers, on the radio, on television, we'd become chronic depressives. But we can read books written by good minds; we can listen to music or watch movies that elate us. We can spend time in nature. We can concentrate on art and beauty.

But everything in our fast-paced world conspires against inner peace. We're losing touch with the natural, normal processes and rhythms of daily life, and this leaves us less time for self-fulfillment. Deteriorating standards and values lead to low self-esteem and rob many of us of our dignity. If we feel an inner emptiness, we will always be tempted by the quick fix, the easy solution, since real life is hard and learning to live fully takes time. But the fact is that we *can* slow things down; we can face our own challenges, however large or small, on terms that are purely ours.

I didn't realize how powerful the impulse against biting the bullet is until a relatively minor but significant accident happened to me. One intensely bright April afternoon, Peter and I were outside, washing our Connecticut house's living room windows. I remember the strong sunlight revealing some streaks on the old glass. I reached to buff the top left-hand windowpane, lost my balance, and fell off the ladder. I laughed it off and tried to get right back up, but something was very wrong. My right knee swelled massively and started throbbing in pain. I'd really hurt myself. At first I thought my knee would heal on its own, but three days later it was sorer than ever.

I called a friend, a hand surgeon who'd recommended a doctor for my back injury years before, and he gave me the name of a young and talented knee specialist. After I was given X rays and a sonogram, Dr. Kelly explained that I'd done damage to my cartilage, and he urged that I have orthoscopic surgery. "It's not an emergency," he said, "but it needs to be done." When I was on the phone with a friend I offhandedly mentioned I needed to have an operation on my knee. "I'll do it when I'm not so busy, possibly in the fall," I casually remarked. From the tone of my voice, my friend immediately picked up on my deeper fear and reluctance about surgery. "It doesn't sound like *you* not to want to get something like this behind you. Don't kid yourself, Sandie. It's not going to get better, and it might get worse." I realized that he was right. I called the doctor's office and requested the first available date for surgery, which was the following week. I must admit that over the next few days I lived in a state of near-panic.

But everything was a whole lot easier than I'd imagined. I came back to the apartment by noon, using hospital-issue crutches. I read in bed before dozing off into a nap. That evening, Peter took me to a bistro, where I had a wonderful dinner and savored a glass of Chardonnay. By the next morning I was able to manage on a cane. The week after my surgery, I flew to Chicago to give a lecture. Who could have kept me from going to see the Monet show at the Chicago Art Institute once I was there? And, by mid-July, my knee operation was history.

What a difference it makes when we're able to face a situation squarely, do what we believe is right, and go forward. What a relief it was to have the inconvenience behind me. And my fall schedule turned out even busier than that of my summer.

Although my knee operation was by no means tragic or life-threatening, the general principle still applies: it is always preferable to get something awful behind you; there's usually something you can do to work through even the most frightening circumstances. No matter how unpleasant a situation, it is *always* better to confront something than to let it fester into a monster.

Destiny is not a matter of chance, it is a matter of choice; it is not a thing to be waited for, it is a thing to be achieved.
—WILLIAM JENNINGS BRYAN

REMAINING SOVEREIGN

Whenever we feel that someone else will take care of us we leave ourselves in unnecessarily vulnerable situations. We must remain sovereign—of our bodies, our minds, and our souls. Anyone who doesn't handle his or her own finances, for example, is asking for trouble. In my business, I've experienced one spouse handling or mishandling the family finances without the knowledge of the other. Oprah Winfrey once sent me a check for $1,500 to cover a small decorating makeover; it was signed by her. When Peter met Oprah and told her how impressed he was about the fact she had signed the check, she told him, "I've been burned, Peter. I like to know where my money goes."

There are certain basic areas in which it's absolutely vital to be informed. As with finances, it's *always* better to know the truth about your health. In one situation I witnessed unfolding, the two—health and money—were in fact strangely connected. A beautiful, talented, ambitious woman, a client of mine, became completely wrapped up in her career as a television journalist. Tanya was dedicated to her work, which consumed most of her time and energy. She decided, out of convenience, to entrust all her finances to her husband, Steve, who was an accountant. His responsibility was to pay the bills. Instead, he played games with his wife's income. He paid or chose not to pay the

Reason is but choosing.

—JOHN MILTON

bills, depending on his mood, but he never discussed anything with Tanya.

When Tanya was having a routine checkup with her
gynecologist, the doctor's assistant told her that her last
office visit had not been paid for. She was asked to please
pay for both visits. Tanya's face flushed. "There must be
a mistake," she said. "We thought it was an oversight at
first," the assistant replied, "but we've sent six statements."
Tanya stood there shocked. But she was also stuck. She
had relinquished her checkbook to her husband, and she
had no more than a few dollars' cash on her since she was
always driven around by the company car service.

When she confronted her husband that evening, his
reaction was casual and cruel. "What's everyone so upset
about? Okay, okay, I'll pay the damn bill, but it seems
ridiculously high for a routine checkup. What a racket."
When what Steve had just said sank in, Tanya burst into
tears. "How could you even *think* you didn't have to pay
my doctor? Dr. Wesler is my doctor and she's also my
friend. I feel violated. Who do you think you are? It's *my*
money!" When Steve nervously laughed and replied,
"What's the big deal? You must be getting your period,"
Tanya's mood changed to rage.

What circumstances would ever make a grown woman,
with a responsible job and a good income, completely ab-
dicate her financial affairs to her husband? How can she
ever treat herself to a present or buy her spouse dinner if
she doesn't have access to her own hard-earned money?
Couldn't she at least carry a purse-size checkbook with
her? Tanya was deeply embarrassed about the unpaid-bill
incident, and subconsciously she didn't want to face the

issue of her dependence on Steve. The result was that she suddenly felt uneasy about going to see her gynecologist. In fact, she put off her next routine examination for several years.

One weekday morning when Tanya was in the shower washing her hair, she felt pain in her right breast when she raised her arm. When she touched the sore spot, she detected a lump, a large, solid mass. Knowing how to examine her own breasts, she palpated her left one, which was normal — a bad sign. She immediately called her office and told them she was going to the doctor. She called Dr. Wesler's assistant and told her about her discovery, and the assistant immediately answered, "Come right down. We'll squeeze you in." After getting dressed, Tanya ran downstairs to the library and rifled through the desk drawers one by one until she found the checkbook. Angrily, she ripped out several checks, threw the checkbook back in the drawer, and rushed out the door.

Without realizing what she'd done, Tanya had taken her life into her own hands. In the intervening time she had had a number of confrontations with Steve, and recently had even considered divorcing him. In the taxi, she experienced hot flashes. All sorts of thoughts began to race around in her head. Was she also going through paramenopause, she wondered, or was it just a nervous attack? She hadn't had a child, and all of a sudden it struck her that at one level she hadn't wanted to have one with Steve. She'd buried her anger toward him by concentrating on her job one hundred percent, but the marriage was definitely strained. And now what if she did have breast cancer? Would she need chemotherapy? Would her hair fall

The ordinary man is involved in action. The hero acts.
—HENRY MILLER

A man's wisdom is most conspicuous where he is able to distinguish among dangers and make choice of the least.
—NICCOLÒ MACHIAVELLI

out? Could she *ever* really forgive Steve, whatever happened?

The diagnosis lived up to her dread. The tumor was malignant and definitely needed to be removed. "How long have you been feeling pain?" Dr. Wesler asked. Crying, Tanya shook her head. "I don't know, a while, I guess." After hearing the news she wanted another opinion. She was stunned, and she also wanted to kill Steve. Dr. Wesler understood and called a top breast surgeon on an emergency basis. Dr. Thompson also agreed to see Tanya early that afternoon. First, she had a mammogram. Hours passed; after reviewing the mammogram, the surgeon explained that it was a fast-growing tumor and needed to be removed right away. "The tumor or my breast?" "I don't know," Dr. Thompson answered. Tanya's worry transformed into shock. Whom could she turn to for help? The last person she thought of was Steve. She called a friend who had had successful nonmalignant surgery. "I need help," she told the friend. "I want to go see *your* breast surgeon."

It was three-thirty by the time Tanya made arrangements to see a third doctor. She called her secretary to say she wouldn't be in until the next morning. The secretary asked if she was all right. Crying, Tanya said, "No," and hung up. When she eventually called Steve's office from the hospital where she was waiting to see her friend's surgeon, she had regained her composure and was cool. But she was really mad. What right did Steve have to withhold paying her doctor in the first place? Tanya was examined and told the same thing she'd heard a few hours earlier

If you want a thing done, go; if not, send.

—BENJAMIN FRANKLIN

1758

from Dr. Thompson. She now began to accept the information.

Tanya had advanced breast cancer and needed major surgery. But she had no idea what her insurance would cover and was on the verge of panic. Oh, no—what if Steve hadn't kept up the health insurance premiums either? What if she was going to have to pay for the operation on her own? She had a mastectomy six days later, by the first surgeon Tanya consulted, Dr. Thompson. Though she was nurtured compassionately by her gynecologist and her surgeon in the painful, unpleasant days ahead, Tanya remained in psychological turmoil. Unable to deal with her disfigurement or the whole reality of what happened, Steve defensively drew away. And Tanya's worst fears were again confirmed. He hadn't paid the insurance premiums. Her premonition had been right.

Tanya lost a breast, and she may lose her life to cancer, but she also gained something important. Her friends were enormously supportive. She had good counseling. But the most significant thing was that she was at last learning to cope as an adult instead of a needy, childlike person who wanted someone else to take care of everything for her.

Her medical insurance is now handled through her television company. Obviously, had she known Steve wasn't keeping up with the payments, she would have arranged for other insurance long before. But now she has learned not to leave anything to others.

Painful surgery ending in disfigurement, plus learning that her spouse had reneged on his financial obligations to manage her money, were a lot for Tanya to swallow at

To be awake is to be alive.

—HENRY DAVID THOREAU

once. But she had empowered herself by instinctively tearing out some blank checks when she first fled her house to go to the doctor's office that dark, stormy Tuesday morning. It was not just her femininity that was being threatened, but her *life;* suddenly she realized how important it was for her to take charge. Being a control freak, Steve was furious when he discovered the missing checks, but not as outraged as Tanya was when she finally woke up to what was going on.

Tanya did need to have chemotherapy. Her hair fell out. She took a leave of absence from her job. She and Steve agreed to separate. In the months that followed, Tanya slowly and painfully grew to realize the extent of her dependence, the lengths she had gone to to avoid facing serious responsibilities. Today she's still hard at work taking care of unmet needs, but she feels she will be able to manage on her own.

Go home, and take care of what you have. Provide places for all your things.
—MOTHER ANN
SHAKER FOUNDER

THE WORST TRAGEDY

Another deeper, more tragic story illustrates how trying it can be, amid great grief, to have the courage and strength to begin healing after biting the bullet. The last words Emily said to her daughter were, "I love you, darling. I'm glad you're home safe." Margaret had been to a debutante party until three in the morning. Still party high, she had brought her date, Bob, back to her apartment. While she and Bob made scrambled eggs and English muffins, they relived the fun evening of friends, dancing, and laughter. When they saw some pink in the sky outside the kitchen window, they decided to go up to the roof and watch the dawn over Chicago, where the family lived.

What happened next meant that the sun would never rise again in the heart of Margaret's mother and father. Margaret somehow fell to her death. Bob, who was looking at the lake on the other side of the roof, didn't even realize what had happened at first. Did her high heel get stuck in the tar, or the hem of her taffeta ball gown? Did she get vertigo and faint? No one would ever know the answer; the only real fact was the most terrible, that Margaret was dead. Her parents were shattered.

Every parent has recurring nightmares of what could happen to their child. We try to teach our children how to be independent and free — we want them to live rich lives, suck at the marrow, dare, be full of adventure, take risks, embrace curiosity. We also want our children safe, protected, and sheltered from the horrors of the real world. Parents sigh deeply when a child comes home safely at night. Crime, drunk driving, and crazies out there make us perpetual worriers. Home is safe. Emily had finally felt free to go to sleep because Margaret had come home.

To lose a child is the most awful, agonizing, horrible grief; it breaks your heart forever, an unbearable pain that scars the soul. Nothing can change that reality. Never can there be a time of greater despair or helplessness, no matter how strong your faith or how courageous you are.

Margaret's funeral service took place three days later. I'd never seen more people packed in the pews. The balcony was filled with school friends. There were exuberant bou-

and hopelessness is to take what we have left and make the most of it.

Emily kept telling me, "I have to be strong for my daughter." And yet her pain seemed to produce in her, over those long months, a deepening appreciation for and love of life. Was Emily trying to live for Margaret? Probably. But, curiously, it was only in Emily's process of building a new life that she felt she and Margaret could be close together. Death's sting never fades, but in a sense that's positive; it is a constant reminder of what we have and what we've lost. Life *must* go on for those who remain alive.

We're woken in the middle of the night and we confront horror, a devastating shock we'll never really get over. It's not television, not a newspaper headline, not your neighbor's child, not your friend's husband, not your colleague's medical report—suddenly, the situation is thrown directly at you. Slam. You wake up, turn on the light. How can you face the reality of it?

What happens to us is *real*, raw, unadorned. How we choose to manage is our only mainstay. The choice we have is how to position ourselves to move through such dark, horrendous times. Death teaches us about life in the same way that darkness shows us the light, and our attitude and spirit make the distinction clear. We can gradually choose which of the two poles—death or life, darkness or light—we will make our own; we learn to allow ourselves to cope.

After many months, Emily was even able to find pleasure in nesting. The parts of her life that she had some control over fell into order. The new apartment grew more charming every day. When you're creating a serene, beau-

Adventure is
worthwhile in itself.
—AMELIA EARHART

tiful environment, your mood is elevated. Beauty is medicine and reduces stress.

I've been to hundreds of celebrations, but the one Emily and David gave for their closest friends, those of us who saw them through this hard time, was the most beautiful I've ever seen. People came from Hawaii, Connecticut, California, New York, Colorado. Everyone came because they *had* to be there for themselves. Emily didn't have to thank us for coming. We, the family friends, were the grateful ones. Why is it that so many of the wisest people in our lives, those who become our teachers, who inspire us to appreciate life more completely, are people who have experienced personal tragedy?

CAREER CHANGES

It's not only when we confront a deadly threat to ourselves or the loss of a loved one that we have to bite the bullet; often the tragedy is that we have to give up something we cherish. A different order of pain is involved, a lesser agony, but it still hurts deeply—and, in many ways, it demands the same sort of courage to overcome as do the worst of life's devastations.

When we celebrated Peter's birthday ten years ago, friends of his since his college days at Yale gathered for dinner at our apartment. We were celebrating a fulfilled life; the photographs taken at the party show Peter beaming with pleasure, contentment, satisfaction, and playfulness.

Three evenings later he came home at eight o'clock, ashen-faced, his shirttails untucked. I couldn't tell at first if he'd been mugged or had suffered a heart attack. His hands were icy. "Let's talk," he whispered in my ear as he hugged me at the front door.

We sat in the living room. I lit a fire and poured two glasses of wine while Peter told me what had happened. I sat there in numb shock. A group of lawyers in the firm he loved, where he'd practiced as a trial lawyer for twenty-six years, had basically told him that quality no longer counted. Winning cases wasn't the game anymore; billable hours was. Milk the client or beat it.

In front of the fire that evening, Peter cried out in pain. His career and everything he stood for professionally seemed ruined. His hands warmed up, but he remained shattered. He had no choice but to leave the firm, since he could never square his values with those of the new management breed. That choice was the only light at the end of the tunnel for Peter. After a long soak in a tub of hot, near-scalding water, he got his color back. Why prolong the pain of loss, he realized, if you can't do anything about it? He went to sleep a free man that night. He spoke with many of his colleagues over the weekend and discussed his situation with friends and family, but inside, he instinctively knew what he had to do.

There was going to be a general meeting the following week, with partners coming to New York from the firm's Florida and Washington offices. Peter prepared himself. At lunch, before the partners had finished their shrimp cocktails, he stood up and said, "Partners, I'm resigning from the firm. But I'm not retiring. I have work to do."

Whatever you choose to do, don't complain.

—ALEXANDRA BRANDON STODDARD

The goal of perfectibility is a bastardized concept smuggled into ethics from technology...

—ROLLO MAY

After distributing his letter of resignation to each of his thirty-five colleagues, Peter left the room, hopped into a taxi, and headed up to 3 East 52nd Street, where I was waiting for him at our all-time favorite restaurant, La Grenouille. We had decided to celebrate the occasion— and his decision—extravagantly. Peter walked in smiling and kissed me. "It's over," he whispered in my ear before being seated. There would be plenty of time after lunch to think about what he'd do next; for now, we were going to forget everything and just enjoy ourselves. Peter had to accept that the firm he'd loved for so long was never going to be the same again, and that the only thing he could honorably do was quit. But the decision was terrifying, too: Highly respected lawyer or not, he was still leaving the security of an established firm, with all the rewards and benefits that went with it, to start out on his own. At age sixty he was taking a step that would leave lawyers half his age sweating.

But what had at first seemed like a blow to the solar plexus turned out to be a blessing. Peter loves practicing law in his small one-partner firm, and he has found that he thrives on the challenge of working complex problems out on his own, without the help of an army of stenographers, legal research assistants, and junior partners. He's set up offices for himself at the apartment and the Connecticut house. He's discovered that he can serve his clients' needs wherever he is; he often sees clients in our living room, which he calls his "uptown office."

Today, a decade later, Peter counts his decision to leave the firm as the best he has ever made in his professional life. Had he stayed, had he not bitten the bullet, he would

> The first act of
> freedom is to
> choose it.
> —WILLIAM JAMES

now be far poorer in spirit than he is. Chances are that he would have retired and given up the law entirely years ago; instead he has been able to remain as passionately committed to his work as ever. The personal and professional blow that at one point seemed unbearable to him is now, in hindsight, what he considers one of the proudest moments of his career.

Action is using your own power.

MOVING ON

Curve balls are thrown at us from unexpected directions. There are times when everything seems all right; then, as if overnight, it all collapses. It doesn't have to be disaster like a fire or flood that awakens us to the need to make tough, healthy decisions. Each changing circumstance compels us to reassess the reality of our lives.

All of us have stories of how we've had to be brave and face the losses life deals us. Losing one's health, one's child, or a beloved job have one common denominator. We're *forced* to let go. In the face of real tragedy, we have every reason to become clinically depressed, but the simple act of doing what has to be done, doing our best with what remains to us, facing the problem and working it through, has a therapeutic value. You can preserve memories, using your creative energy to rebuild your life and help others facing similar tragedies. By moving on, you transcend the emotional crisis. You may begin to work in the hope of preventing similar tragedies from happening to anyone else; you may find people in the same situation turning to you for advice. But whatever you do, you'll find that your example becomes a resource to others.

Another positive is that our appreciation for what we have, and have had in the past, is always curiously deepened once we act to face adversity. Things aren't always clear at first, but time heals emotional scars, providing space for new insights that lead us toward the new and the previously untried. No one wants any pain, dread, and rupture in his or her life, or in the lives of family or friends. But it is a well-known truth that spiritual growth arises from the darkest moments.

If we can continue to take risks, exploring as many creative opportunities as possible, we can be grateful when things work out. But when circumstances change, when things are no longer working, when we're faced with really frightful situations, ones we can hardly believe—these are the very times when we're called upon to be resolute. We have powerful examples all around us of strong-willed people who inspire us to overcome our suffering, even in our worst suffering.

One definition of "to choose" is "to settle," to come to a conclusion. When we decide, we're freed from ambiguity. We don't have to live in perpetual fear and equivocation, worrying about what our next challenging choice will be. What we can decide to do is gather the tools we need and move on. We can ask ourselves, "What can *I* do?" But our task is to be prepared, to be ready to pick the right path when the time comes, no matter how hidden it may at first seem. Ask yourself what your choices are. But once you know, once you see and understand, then you *have* to do

...when human beings think *too* carefully and minutely about an action to be taken, they cannot make up their minds in time to act.

—ALAN W. WATTS

something. The consequences of indecisiveness and inaction can be disastrous. If we fail to choose to handle any situation, it will never be resolved.

Whether you've been hit over the head with harsh reality or you've grown to understand a truth after a long, painful struggle, once you know what you must do, *do* it. Don't be afraid. Life goes on. The world doesn't stop. Pick up the pieces, face the obstacles, and act. Your choice is your way to protect yourself; you transform loss into gain.

PART
TWO

4

$\mathcal{P}$ARENTS AND $\mathcal{S}$IBLINGS

"No one can legislate affection or approval."

—HENRY LOUIS GATES, JR.

BEING PARENTED

Because of their respect for their own parents and their recognition of my love for mine, my mentors have helped me to understand my mother and father more thoroughly. I loved my parents more than anyone else until, in the sweep of time, my deepest love was transferred to my spouse and, later, my own children.

We don't choose our parents, but once we've become adults we have the choice of how we are going to react to them. We don't always agree with our parents, but this doesn't mean we always have to argue and fight about our disagreements. But there are times when we will. Our ages, our relative maturity, and our circumstances make us view things differently. Chemistry, genetics, health, environment, fate, and faith make the parent-child relationship complex. Its feelings run deep and are delicate, volatile, and ever-changing, and each relationship is individual and multifaceted. We run from hot to cold, depending on a large number of factors that have little or nothing to do with the deeper, constant love we feel between us. Both sides should display some tolerance if parents and children are to affirm each other. Gratitude must go both ways in order for mutual understanding to develop. If we each take responsibility for our own lives, if we have faith in ourselves so we can change what needs to be corrected, we can forget the real and imagined hurts our parents have inflicted on us, and we can give ourselves permission to be thankful to them.

As Peter and I travel around the country, we're heartened by the great majority of people we see who have healthy relationships with their parents, living or dead. But we don't have to watch television or listen to the radio or read newspapers, magazines, and books to know that there is violence, abuse, and destruction in far too many families. We can look around our communities, our own neighborhoods, our immediate friends, to know how much pain and agony there is. We recognize the personal pain inflicted on us by our own parents.

But the fact is that we relate to the world according to our relationship with our parents. My daughter Alexandra read a letter in an Ann Landers column recently that protested against children chronically blaming their parents for all their problems. The woman who wrote the letter went on to say that your mother might have been an alcoholic, but she brought you into this world. If not for

Nobody who has not been in the interior of a family can say what the difficulties of any individual of that family may be.

—JANE AUSTEN

your parents, you wouldn't be here. The word "dysfunctional" seems to be in vogue, although I hate the negative way it sounds. To go through life single-mindedly focusing on the shortcomings of our parents is, in most cases, too much. The fact is that because we have parents, we are given life.

No one chooses their parents. We're born out of passion between a man and a woman; it's the luck of the draw from conception. Some of us were planned and wanted; others were mistakes. Some women marry when they become pregnant; others have the child out of wedlock. These are the personal choices our parents made. However, even if parents wish to create us in their image or make us grow into someone we're not, there are natural, biological limits to what they can do to mold us. Many of us have a father who treated a daughter like a son because he wanted a son. Accept it. You didn't do anything to let him down, but your father had expectations that couldn't be fulfilled. Our parents choose how they accept us; we decide how we accept ourselves. It's true that for every child who looks up to his or her parents, there are many others who condemn them, often justifiably. But to endlessly complain shows a reluctance to let go and move on.

If either your parents or stepparents have truly abused you, you no longer have an obligation to honor them. They violated the privilege of parenting you. As an adult you are no longer responsible to them. You're an orphan; you're free.

Yet it's neither cleansing nor therapeutic to try to defend yourself by "telling all" about your parents. There has been a rash of mama and papa bashing in juicy block-

Serve as an example: choose not to assert your will on others.

Life goes by—
choose how!

busters recently, and I don't think this is a healthy trend. I know that some therapists urge their patients to "write it down" as a sort of emotional pressure valve, but even psychiatrists create composites when they write case studies, changing names to protect individual privacy. Yet these celebrities believe they must go public with their private family lives. Whom does it help? How can it be warranted? If a child has been run through the mill by his mother or father and is compelled to tell a uniquely gruesome story, my feeling is that it would be more graceful to make it fiction, and write under a pseudonym.

What's difficult to face is that we're usually cut from the same cloth as our parents. When we put them down, we diminish ourselves. Even if someone has certifiably rotten parents, where is one's sense of self-pride? Anger toward a mother or a father, no matter how excusable, ultimately becomes an expression of self-loathing. Anger is temporary insanity; until we choose to let go of it, we'll never be free to build a different, less troubled life.

There are enough examples to illustrate how a great individual can overcome the bleakest lack of parental care (or worse) and still flourish. On the other hand, we've all known extraordinarily fine parents who gave their all to their children, only to suffer the disappointment of having raised ungrateful, unproductive parasites. There are no hard-and-fast rules to parenting, and all the best-selling how-to books that claim there are don't seem to have produced a new generation of happy, well-adjusted families. There are many factors involved in the vitally important relationship between parent and child, but the only constant in successful families is a mutual sense of obligation.

Our misery is not *always* our parents' fault, any more than our parents' parents were in turn always to blame for *their* unhappiness. The sooner we look within ourselves and face our own problems, the quicker we can take positive steps to make useful choices that will improve our lives; after all, no family is perfect. Whenever we feel we can't cope alone, we seek help. But even the choice to ask for help has to come from inside ourselves.

We're always free to make choices about how we're going to live our lives. If you feel you've been given short shrift or a really grim deal, comfort yourself that you will choose to behave differently with your own children. In other words, choose *not* to subject a child to the same kind of life you experienced growing up.

Remember that our parents were once children who had similar feelings about *their* parents, too, so that if we can look at the relationship from the other side, reversing our roles, we will greatly increase the scope of our vision. Our whole life should be an attempt to make the most of what we've already been given. This is our only true inheritance. The relationship between parents and children is about passages, and some of them will inevitably be rough. Parents would be far more tolerant of their children if they opened themselves up to the fact that they were not only children once, but occasionally brats.

All interesting voyages involve hardships and hurdles. When parents act as though they never wet their bed or got caught with their hand in the cookie jar, they tend to

...the self is the
sum of the different
roles the
person plays.
—WILLIAM JAMES

❖

be far less tolerant of their children's mistakes. Parents who suffer from selective amnesia are being unloving to their child. We will always make errors. I was once at a party given by a young couple I know. At one point, their six-year-old son came racing down the stairs and ran into his mother, who dropped two of the Waterford glasses she was carrying. The son was obviously horrified by what he had done and burst into tears. I was thrilled to see what happened next: Instead of scolding the boy, his mother instead told him—and a delighted audience of adults— about the time when she as a young girl had broken not two, but six of her mother's favorite glasses. Not only do we mess up here and there, the boy learned, but our parents do too.

When parents demonstrate unqualified love, a child can get back on track faster; when parents act in controlling, judgmental ways, they create feelings of insecurity in the child, a sense that the child has let his or her parents down. But the reality is that we should be far more concerned about not letting ourselves down, since our wholeness is the only legacy we will leave to our children. We can love without blame. We wish we could change things, but we can't. Yet by accepting our parents as they are, we can adjust to them.

THE GREATEST GIFT

My life has been enriched by a number of strong and sensitive men and women who believed in me and gave me confidence in my own abilities, yet who had no parental obligations toward me. A parent-child relationship has the same fluctuating contradictions, the yin-yang, that exist in all real relationships. Ideally, parents should be strong, in order to set an example, yet at the same time sensitive to the weaknesses in themselves and their children. No one else, no mentor, no aunt, no role model or stepmother will ever love you as much as your parents, or expose themselves more vulnerably to you. It takes a very long time to figure all this out, for parent as well as child. Because of our parents' responsibility, as well as authority, they often act in less obviously loving ways, perhaps, than mentors do, but their love is their greatest gift to us. The mentor relationship is usually conducted from a safe distance, and it lacks the built-in obligation to stick by us when we're not at our best. A parent's love is both unqualified *and* a lifetime commitment.

Alexandra has made a friend of a mother of five children who runs a pizza restaurant in Prince William County, Virginia, where Alexandra goes with her newspaper colleagues. This woman told Alexandra that since she gave birth to her first child, she hasn't stopped worrying. "That's a parent's job, to worry about their kids.

Do not let time pass without accomplishing something. Otherwise you will regret it when your hair turns gray.

—YUE FEI

dependence with a needy parent around, since in such cases the child often has to act the role of the parent. Marsha regularly gave her mother money. But because Marsha was establishing a life with Sam, Penny felt excluded: her only child was abandoning her. Marsha chose Sam; she did nothing wrong. The best thing she can do for herself now is not to give in to her mother's whiny, manipulative, self-pitying ways. Penny's lack of self-reliance tainted her relationship with the one person she loved most. Marsha now has to learn to honor and respect her mother without trying to satisfy her every need. It's hard, but her choice is clear. If she didn't put some distance between herself and her mother, she could not give her undivided attention to nurturing her own marriage and her new baby, George.

No matter how compelling the demands may be, we can't give more than we are able. If Penny could step aside and see how much stress and pressure she's causing Marsha, she'd surely back off. But from her narrow point of view, she sees Marsha's behavior as selfish, thoughtless, disloyal, and unappreciative.

It's difficult for anyone to ever let go, especially parents. To a parent, a child is *always* a child. Right up until the end, when Mother sat in the reclining chair in her hospital room, even while slipping into an irreversible coma a few weeks before her death, she acted out the role of my advisor, teacher, the authority figure in my life, as though the umbilical cord had never been cut.

I appreciate so many aspects of my life now without having a mother constantly trying to improve me. I'm sure the instruction was helpful; I learned a great deal under the discipline of Mother's exacting standards, as well as from her corrections—but now I can breathe a sigh of relief knowing she won't see the cobwebs on the windowsills or be shocked by a less than perfectly made bed. What's ironic is that I know she made a tremendous effort not to be a burden to me. I remember the last words Mother spoke to me: "Go home to Peter and the girls."

With both my parents dead, I'm an adult orphan, like so many of us. Having your parents die forces you to feel grown-up. You are your own person and you're on your own. Yet I'll always be my parents' child; we never bury our childhood or our yearning to be cared for.

At the same time, I am also the parent of two young adults. Alexandra and Brooke are no longer children; they have grown up and left home, and now they are living full, vital, independent lives. For me to fool myself into thinking that they still need me to teach them right from wrong, to inculcate certain values in them, to tell them what to do, would be to retard their growth and overstep my boundaries as a parent.

It's true that our identities as parents become clouded when our children grow up and we're suddenly faced with the antithesis of what we've always done, which was feed, shelter, nurture, provide, care for, educate, discipline, and protect; now our role is to love and let go. A parent's instinct to hover around an adult son or daughter is not only selfish but inappropriate. In family life, we should be completely present until the child becomes an adult. Our role should then become clear. At approximately eighteen the child goes off to college or gets a job. Physical and emotional separation will automatically occur, which is healthy and natural. Parents should embrace a child who breaks

> ...guiding without interfering...If you keep your mind from judging...
> —LAO-TZU

away, who takes risks, who dares to build his own life. To take flight, every child needs a boost from his or her parents; but, judging from reality, to willingly let children out of captivity to fend for themselves is a very difficult thing to do. Parents try, but the process is rocky and filled with an equal measure of breakthroughs and outbursts. Heraclitus tells us that everything is flux, that nothing stays static. This is especially true with parents and children: the dynamics of the relationship is a heady brew of contradictions, inconsistencies, and mixed feelings.

Only when we no longer have a great need for the nurturing support of our parents will we be able to choose to love them as individuals in their own right.

—AARON STERN

RAISING CHILDREN

Carl Jung talks about the conflict of duties. We have a duty to honor and obey our parents—but what if they're not wholly honorable? What if we have to listen to our own voice, which is quite alien, even unacceptable, to our parents? Look back at the choices your parents made, at what they hold dear. How different are your values from theirs? Likewise, parents have to look at their beliefs and reevaluate them in light of what their children believe in, value, and need in an entirely different world.

Parents should come to realize that they can't judge their adult children without taking their individuality and their world into consideration. Parents can try to openly communicate, but they can't expect their grown children to tell them *all* their secrets. The challenge for parents and their adult children is thus to begin afresh, with new definitions and boundaries. We can choose how we're going to react to our parents and our children, seeking out new attitudes and perspectives, recognizing that our responsibilities to each change with time.

After all, each of our lives has to be understood, interpreted, and lived individually. An ideal parent nourishes, sustains, and supports the child and empowers him or her to be self-sufficient and open to growth. Once they let go, all parents can ever hope for or expect is for their children to be themselves, to seize life with all the energy, vision, and talent they possess, and believe in themselves and the world around them.

The time to spend with your children is when they're living at home, before they go off to college or start on a career. This time can never be recovered. If a parent is asleep during these important years, no amount of guilt or attention later will take the place of having been there for a child. When a parent puts business before his child, for instance, he kids himself by saying he'll make it up to the child later. A child might say she understands, but she begins to get the idea that other things are more important than her. A parent has to look at the big picture when choosing where to be when a conflict in scheduling comes up. *Being* there when a child needs you is emotionally healing and loving.

The bond between parent and child is far from a given; it has to be worked on. By spending unpressured time together, parents see and hear what makes the child happy. If a parent doesn't put the time in just being there, listening, he won't sense what his child is all about. All too often, parents have misguided expectations for their children, and

Truth exists only as the individual himself produces it in action.

—SØREN KIERKEGAARD

Each one of us lives
as it were in a private
world of his own.
—RENÉ DUBOS

the pressure they exert can be devastating. While a junior at Spence School in New York City, Alexandra was taking a Latin exam when a proctor caught a friend of hers cheating. He dismissed her from school. When the child got home, her mother was in the living room, chairing a meeting of one of her many committees. The child pretended she didn't feel well; she walked past the group of women and down the hall to her parents' bathroom. She locked herself in and rampaged through the medicine cabinet, swallowing every pill in sight. Luckily, she survived: Her mother found her and called an ambulance just in time. But the pressure she felt because of college boards, the SATs, and college applications had been too much. Her father had insisted she go to Stanford. Needless to say, she didn't. She dropped out of school and needed intensive psychiatric help.

If the young girl's parents had let her cry out in frustration, or talk the problem over and get it off her chest, no doubt she would not have felt compelled to go to such desperate lengths to send them the message. The fact is that our children are more than willing to communicate their problems to us. There's no need for us to go through their drawers, open their letters, or read their journals; if we listen to them and treat them with the same respect we accord our adult friends, they will tell us when they need — or don't need — our help.

It's true that teenage children in the nest aren't fifty-fifty partners with their parents. Children don't have automatic rights to equality; the privilege is earned over time, with the child's increasing maturity. But after the formative years are over, parents should let go of the reins and become friends with their children. This can be one of the greatest times of our lives.

Because of the current economic climate, our children don't have the same advantages children in previous generations had. Since they can't afford to pay rent and survive on their own without drastically lowering their standard of living, many of them are returning home to live with their parents long after they've emotionally left the nest. Yet once a child-adult is emancipated, it is a mistake for parents to keep the same assumptions they had when the child was in the nest and still very much a part of the family life.

For the first eighteen years, parents can instill in their children the values that will help them cope with life. After a child is free, that responsibility is largely over. How many parents are prepared for this transition? Awareness that it will happen can make all the difference between a beneficial separation and an awkward, hurtful alienation. The bond of acceptance, sensitivity, and gratitude between parent and child is a mirror; if parents are there for their child, chances are the child will grow up to adulthood to feel the same sense of obligation, responsibility, and commitment to the parents.

Many parents who enjoyed raising their children become dependent on caring for and nurturing them long after it's appropriate. There could be many reasons to cling too tightly: a parent is divorced, widowed, or locked in an empty marriage held together for the sake of the children. A parent's sickness—either emotional or physical—can also put a strain on the child.

A parent should thus try to be as complete a person as

possible. I don't believe it's healthy for any adult to live solely for the relationship with another person. A mother can't live *for* her son or a father *for* his daughter. Each of us has to have a full life, things we love to do for our own sake that have nothing to do with our children. We have to have a developed self *before* we can take care of a child. When an airplane is in trouble, the mother is told to put her oxygen mask on before she puts one on her child.

So it's healthy for parents to realize they have only a score of years of child-rearing and to anticipate and plan for a rich new chapter in their lives after the children leave home. A young adult son who received loving care while growing up will rejoice in his parents' living a full, busy life. From college age on, he will want to make his own plans, have fun with his own friends, and live his own life without feeling guilty that he's abandoning his poor, lonely, pathetic parents. When a mother is too effusive with a grown child, the child has no choice—she just wants to get out of there. When there isn't any pressure or guilt, parents and their young adult children can have a great deal of fun together. Accepting the metamorphosis of a child into an attractive, mature adult permits the relationship to be more equal.

Emancipated children see their parents in an entirely different light. No longer mortified to be caught dead with them, the children discover how wise, intelligent, interesting, and humorous their mother and father can be. Depending on the grown child's own sense of well-being and self-confidence, he or she actually becomes proud of them.

Because the parent-child relationship is so involved and complex, however, it's almost a given that some psycho-

Life only demands of you the strength you possess. Only one feat is possible, not to have run away.

—DAG HAMMARSKJÖLD

106

logical loose ends are left dangling long after the child has grown into an adult. The healthiest way to cope with these unresolved issues is to do it before the parent's serious illness or death. If you felt abandoned as a child, your parent's death could cause you to feel anger and frustration—at your parent for once more leaving you in the lurch, and at yourself for not having taken action in time. It's healing to just visit a parent with whom you've experienced some resentment, and be forgiving. What you say isn't as important as the fact that you are there in a generous, loving way. By letting go of anger or resentment, you open the relationship up to mutual love and support.

If you suffered from jealousy as a child because you believed your mother loved your sibling more than you, you could be *dead* right. In any family, each parent has a special connection to a particular child; although some parents may deny this truth, it's only human. Sometimes the bond is influenced by the order of birth. The oldest, for instance, tends to be the test run; parents tend to be more insecure, nervous, and strict with their first child. No parents are saints, but that doesn't mean yours didn't love you. Perhaps you wouldn't have received more love had your parents never given birth to your siblings. In any case, you won't improve your spirit by dwelling on something you can't change now.

Parents and children alike go through difficult times, and they can both survive them. For a child, the very fact that his or her parents have changed their lives around, out of necessity but for the better, is a shining testament to possibility. It's never too late for parents to make amends to their children, and as children we in turn can

You have to choose the voice you are going to trust. You can't listen to everyone.

—ALICE HOFFMAN

learn to be forgiving and tolerant after we've been hurt or let down by a parent who, for whatever reason, was incapable of fully loving us.

PARENTING OUR PARENTS

Especially now that our parents are living longer than ever, I believe that we should assume a certain responsibility for them. I'm not insisting that we take our elderly parents into our home if they have a disease that requires professional care. While some of us do, many have arranged for other alternatives; it is not necessary to have a parent live under your *own* care. What *is* important is that you check to see that they are being properly cared for, or make arrangements for a sibling who lives nearer to assume this duty. The Old Testament enjoins us to honor our mother and father. Just because a parent has Alzheimer's or some other form of senility doesn't mean that he or she should be abandoned.

Choosing to do the right thing in this respect should not be a gender question, but it often is. Some are far more likely to wait until a parent is in a coma or at death's door before they awaken to the fact that their mother or father is dying, while daughters tend to accept responsibility for the whole process of care-giving. But it's *every* child's obligation to do what they can, to be there. Responsibility shouldn't follow gender lines; daughters are no more likely than sons to enjoy changing bedpans.

I was fortunate in being able to help both my parents before they died. My mother died of lung cancer that metastasized to her bones and brain. I had ten and a half months to spend with her, trying, in whatever way I could, to bring her some joys, to relieve her from the indignity of being in a decaying body racked with excruciating pain. I never felt I could do enough, and I exhausted myself trying. My minister was helpful one morning when he asked me if I was all right. I burst into tears: "No. I'm not all right. My mother's dying." Alan comforted me, then told me something very important: I couldn't "death watch," or focus exclusively on the process of her dying. Alan was right. It wasn't the regular trips to the hospital in Connecticut that were draining me; I actually felt at peace when I was there with her at her bedside. What was unnerving was the stress of watching my mother disintegrate, hour by hour, in a torturous agony with no hope of recovery.

In those final months I was experiencing how shattering it is to watch the person who brought us into the world enter into the final, uncomfortable days of life.

After realizing how true what Alan told me was, I was able to concentrate on her strength and amazing bravery. I was aware that there was no way I could make up the time later. I now have rich memories of her, and wherever I go, I recall, consciously or subconsciously, the tenderness that passed between us during her last days. Whatever disagreements we'd ever had became irrelevant. We both chose to concentrate on our love and mutual respect. Toward the end, the heavy doses of morphine she was given allowed her to prepare herself for death. Little by little, she moved away, into another world, a place I could not go.

But the bravest are surely those who have the clearest vision of what is before them, glory and danger alike, and yet notwithstanding go out to meet it.

—THUCYDIDES

We will never fully understand its mystery, but just to treasure family love, to feel the sense of continuity, and to know that we chose to be *there*, to enjoy all of its richness, is reward enough.

SIBLING RELATIONSHIP

Like our parents, who our siblings are is no choice of ours. Our ideal as good, decent, kind people is to love them; most of us feel embarrassed if we don't. In real life, this is too often the case.

Sibling rivalry is an instinctive, innate phenomenon. Yet while it is universal, it doesn't have to last forever. My brother Powell, who is five years older than me, has been a loving, protective presence throughout my life. From my early childhood memories of him tenderly brushing my hair to our close, affectionate relationship today, we've shared a living bond that continues to grow deeper with the years. Every family has success stories, siblings whose relationships are consciously based on equality, understanding, and reciprocity.

So what are our choices? How can we grow to become ourselves and yet get along with siblings who have different attitudes and interests?

I haven't had the easiest time with my siblings, and I've spent most of my life thinking this was a personal flaw. But I've let go of this feeling in the past few years because I've stopped blaming myself or my sister or brothers. Like an arranged marriage, siblings are people thrust upon each other in a close, intense environment and are expected to work things out.

We should all try to bring out the best in others. Whether it's with a sister, a brother, or a friend, any relationship can be constructive or destructive or both, depending on the circumstances. But no one can force two sisters to be best friends, two brothers to get along, or a brother to adore his older or younger sister. Mutual respect and love is a combination of luck and will. One without the other isn't enough.

A big part of growing up is to accept our siblings as they are, and accept how they decide to live their lives. But none of us has to give in to their choices at the expense of our own goals and freedom. We can choose to direct our own fate. Just because you have a sister or brother you don't like to spend time with doesn't mean you are disloyal or selfish.

When two people are lovable, a special bond is possible, but it is *not* automatic. If you don't get along with a sibling, it doesn't necessarily mean that you are an awful person and that you should assume all the blame. On the contrary. It could be that the two of you are just not compatible, that you don't really enjoy being together; in fact, your sibling could just plain be a drag. When you feel you lose more than you gain from a sibling, you can restrict your contacts once you are an adult.

Nor are you necessarily responsible for the ways a sibling acts in later life, the decisions he or she chooses to make. In an atmosphere where one child thrives, another may not be able to function. After a long struggle to cope,

It's only by forgetting about yourself that you draw near to God.

—HENRY DAVID THOREAU

my younger brother committed suicide. No one can ever know the depths of pain in another person's soul. Long before my brother killed himself, he chose many self-destructive paths. He became incapable of making wise decisions for himself; he lost his freedom to make choices. His dependence on medication and institutions destroyed him. Life not only lost its meaning but became unbearable to him.

Do I have any idea of the depth of my brother's pain? No — I can't begin to understand. Do I wonder why Chip, why not me? I was the third child, Chip was the baby. Do I blame my parents? Did the way they acted toward us as children have a fatal effect on him that it didn't have on me? Do I feel that I abandoned my baby brother when I went off to boarding school? Could I have done something to try to save his life? Do I feel responsible? I loved Chip, and these aren't easy questions. After many years of trying to answer them, however, I finally realized that I never would be able to. Chip was my brother, but he was also an independent human being, with motivations and thoughts I never knew and never could know. There was nothing I could do to change him; that was *his* responsibility, and he chose not to do it. All I could ever do is love him, grieve, and let go.

Each of us must eventually make our own choices in order to live a life in accordance with our beliefs and interests. I see no reason why we should feel responsible for the choices of a sibling any more than they should concern themselves with ours.

We all have poignant stories about siblings. My mother, for example, was terrified of her older sister, Cath-

I took them to the edge and they were afraid. I took them to the edge and they were very afraid. I took them to the edge and I pushed them and they flew.

—NINETEETH-CENTURY FRENCH POET

erine, who patronized her and constantly claimed to be intellectually superior to her. If we have inherited a sibling whose grain goes against ours, chances are there will be friction. What are our choices? Siblings are, after all, different from stepchildren. When we choose a spouse who has children, we assume a certain responsibility toward them, even when they act in unloving, unthoughtful ways. We don't relish it; all we can do is cope. But if your sister takes advantage of you or causes you deep emotional pain, I see no reason to see her until her attitude changes. Treat your brother and sister the way you treat friends. A friend is someone with whom you can be yourself, share your most intimate thoughts as well as celebrate life's exalted moments, and feel loved and accepted.

Our sisters and brothers know us very well—how to please us as well as how to hurt us. They know what buttons to press. Children can be cruel to each other in the struggle to share the same physical and emotional space. But once sisters and brothers grow up, move away, and begin to live separate lives, the relationship is bound together only by mutual trust and respect; if not, it disintegrates. Even siblings who really loved and adored each other can run into unexpected difficulties, hurts, and resentments.

You can't be friends with a brother or sister who takes advantage of you. Your choice is to keep your distance. You can argue that life is short, that you should make up and move on, but if you don't trust a sibling, it's extremely hard to love him or her. Tolerance is different from love and respect. I've seen dozens of people put up with siblings in a cordial manner when they meet at family reunions,

Life is a process: Choices are our tools.

weddings, or funerals, but the relationship is guarded at best. Respect and love are the only basis for a warm bond.

The ideal, the nice choice, isn't always possible. A lingering sadness in my life is that my older sister and I have chosen not to keep seeing each other. It was a tough choice for us both. For now, we are better off living our own separate lives. Due to a complicated set of circumstances that goes back to when we were children, we are a bad mix. I am not good for her; my sister is not good for me. Had we met as adults, we wouldn't have chosen to be friends. I don't want to blame her, but I've come to terms with myself and my limits. When equality and reciprocity are missing, there is no true relationship to hold on to. Our lifestyles were dissimilar, and as the years went on mine seemed to increasingly irritate her. At times she let me know, in no uncertain terms, how she *really* felt about me, which was devastating to me. I know I have many faults — but I didn't know I was *that* awful!

Statistics show that more than half of all siblings don't like each other. I have clients, sisters, who cannot be together. After decades of trying to change her older sister's behavior, the younger sister, Sharon, finally refused to put up with Megan's continual abuse. It wasn't until years later, when Sharon married and had a baby, that she could admit to herself how deeply her sister hurt her. Yet if you listen to Megan's side of the story, you hear that she has bent over backward for her younger sister. The few times they were forced to be together in the same room, the tension was high enough that everyone in the room could feel it. Both women are convinced they're right. Megan is stubborn enough to hold out indefinitely. Unless both choose to change, they are better off not being together. As a friend of mine, Amanda Howard, recently told me, family is an accident. Having a sister you didn't choose or wouldn't select as a friend shouldn't interfere with your well-being. Once we leave home and are on our own, our siblings should not feel free to voice their opinions to us indiscriminately. Most of what you do with your life is no one else's business. If someone acts aggressive and pries into your life, you don't have to give in. Good friends listen and wait for you to talk.

Whenever you do things differently from your family, you always become suspect. The family picks away at you to make you shape up and act like them. A sibling feels he or she knows what will make you happy when, in reality, only you can be the judge. If a sibling were a friend, you would feel absolutely comfortable saying that you appreciate his or her concern, but that you are doing what you feel is best for you. If you have a sibling who is controlling and manipulative, you will probably choose to keep that relationship at arm's length. If you shared a room as a child with a sister or brother, you had no choice. They saw you naked, they had access to your friends, your clothes, your things. Your sibling was thrust upon you. You could have few secrets. But when you're an adult, you're free to choose the people you want to surround yourself with, people who stimulate you in constructive ways.

This doesn't mean that you can't have an occasional family gathering where you remember the best of the good old days. This continuity, when provided in a mutually

> A person whose choices reflect the capacity to care for others more than fifty percent of the time would be a primarily loving human being.
>
> —AARON STERN

accepting manner, is an important way to understand ourselves better. But you should also choose to protect your chosen family—yourself, your spouse and children—from unconstructive interference from relatives.

MONEY ISSUES

Financial independence helps avoid extra complications in the already delicate relationship among siblings; money is a complex issue, and potentially very explosive when it enters into family relationships. When a friend of mine was disappointed by the dishonesty of one of his co-workers, his mother said to him, "Charles, people are *funny* about money."

Patterns often develop in childhood and don't change over the years. One sibling is a saver, for example, while the other is a spender; one works hard, the other is an inveterate moocher. When siblings go into business together, they should be aware of the problems money issues can present. Two clients I admire did choose to invest together as brothers, but they made sure neither would ever regret their financial arrangements. They decided that each was free to make any business arrangements he wished; when they both were co-venturers on a deal, however, they drew up a contract outlining the limits of the arrangement. To further assure mutual trust, their records were maintained at their lawyer's office, where they were kept up to date by an accountant. At any time, day or night, with no notice, either brother could examine the books.

After nearly twenty years of being partners in a number of interesting, successful ventures, the brothers are now reaping the fruits of their business decisions. Everything is still kept clearly spelled out, and both brothers feel comfortable and mutually trusting. Neither ever gave up the checkbook, a smart business decision.

The time siblings most often have to face money issues is when a parent falls seriously ill or dies. Entitlement is a sensitive issue, especially for sisters. After having taken care of an aging parent for years, a woman often finds herself uncompensated. Even if her inheritance were to equal that of her brothers, in a sense it has already been diminished; her brothers will probably neither assume their share of the care-giving nor recognize its value in probate court. This frankly is not fair. Each of us should earn our place in the family, based on our genuine contribution. How nice it would be to have rewards based on merit, and nothing else.

> We are called to be
> choice-makers.
> —REV. SPENCER M. RICE

WHEN YOU'RE LUCKY

I never felt a lack of love, especially not on my mother's part, and I hope my brothers and sister felt some of the same security that I did while growing up. This feeling has sustained me all my life. As I said before, feelings that our parents favored a sister or a brother don't serve us well as adults; the child that is easy to love might not get the same attention as a child in need, but the love is still there. I never felt smothered as a third child, but I did feel important, valuable, and worthy of whatever time and nurturing my parents gave me.

As parents, we can't control the relationship between our children, but sometimes we're just lucky. Alexandra and Brooke have grown closer each year since they were little. When Brooke was four and Alexandra almost seven, they first flew together to California to visit their father. I went on board with them until a stewardess told me I had to deplane. The girls had each other. As I cried, kissing them good-bye, leaving with a lump in my throat—the kind that doesn't go away for two days—I realized they were holding hands, happy, excited about their trip. Now, twenty years later, they share a mutual respect and fondness; they have fun together. I know that it's rare for siblings to find this genuine love for each other, but when it exists, it sets a high, hopeful standard of what is possible.

Those of us who have close, loving ties with a sibling are the exception, not the norm. If you treasure your relationship with your relatives, you are fortunate. When you are on the same beam, no matter how different you are, you are capable of lifting each other up in ways that add depth and texture to the fabric of your life. When you're lucky and things work out, count your blessings.

Happiness is a
conscious choice.

5
*S*POUSES

"For one human being to love another: that is perhaps the most difficult of all our tasks, the ultimate, the last test and proof, the work for which all other work is but a preparation."

—RAINER MARIA RILKE

CHOOSING TO MARRY

To marry or not is a choice, as staying married or getting a divorce has become increasingly a choice that people must face. My aunt, Ruth Elizabeth Johns, a pioneering international social worker, chose not to marry. The daughter of a Methodist minister, she started her career after graduating from Radcliffe and completing her studies at a seminary in Massachusetts. I lived with Aunt Betty for a semester while I was at the New York School of Interior Design. One night at dinner, I asked her why she never married. Her eyes were as deep-set as mine, a family trait, and they seemed grave as she told me her story.

"Only one person asked me to marry him, dear; he was a dentist in Philadelphia. My work takes me all over the world, and I wanted to be free to pursue my career. I understood that my decision meant I would not have my own children, but I have my nieces and nephews as well as my work, which fulfills me. I feel fortunate I am able to travel as much as I do. My choice not to marry has worked out well for me."

Marriage, the ultimate union between two people, certainly isn't for everyone. My aunt was as content with her life as anyone I know. As a woman, her options were limited. She couldn't, in the 1930s, be a minister, so she chose to be a social worker. She reminds me of Ralph Waldo Emerson, who, radical in his beliefs about God, was not invited back to preach in the pulpit, so he took his talks out on the road, calling them speeches rather than sermons and giving them Mondays through Saturdays. Aunt Betty had a mission and preached her sermons in the United Nations as well as the International YMCA and the World Council of Churches.

When I was young I snickered at the fact that she, a single woman, was a marriage counselor. I've learned now that I was wrong. She saw enough in the relationships around her to have plenty of knowledge. No matter how kind and gentle her prospective dentist husband was, Betty Johns would have felt stifled living in conventional Philadelphia. She knew her limits. By not marrying, she gave up any expectation of becoming a mother. This cleared the way for her to focus in earnest on her career.

I feel that I richly benefited from not only having lived and traveled around the world with her, but from being her friend. I've written about my aunt before, so I won't repeat myself, but I feel she had a larger vision or mission.

Only in grammar can you be more than perfect.

—WILLIAM SAFIRE

Not everyone is cut from the same cloth. Aunt Betty was able to influence thousands of children through her work, both in America and all over Southeast Asia. Just as marriage isn't right for everyone, being a mother or father isn't either.

To marry or not to marry? You choose to say yes to this covenant because you love someone so much that you want his or her companionship, to share your lives, to pledge togetherness through sickness and health until death. After you make this life-changing choice, you will face hundreds of other major choices as partners. Why does someone choose to marry? For some, marriage is a tradition: You create a family, establish a stable home, settle down, protect your children, create your own history.

Many of us believe that our spouse is literally our other half. When two people are in the kind of love that deepens and expands over time, the marriage can have the sweetness of a glass of good port. But what makes one marriage work and another become a battlefield? Why do so many marriages fail?

When you fall in love with someone, your passion is all-encompassing. You have no choice. You become a different person. You walk on air, stand tall, feel enabled, feel valuable, feel empowered. We don't intellectualize about who will be our mate for life.

When the match is right for both people, there is reason to expect a lasting, beautiful union. As Carl Jung taught, "The meeting of two personalities is like the contact of two chemical substances: if there is any reaction, both are transformed." But what happens when you marry the wrong person for you, the wrong type? Rather than the

> The meeting of two personalities is like the contact of two chemical substances: if there is any reaction, both are transformed.
>
> —CARL JUNG

chemical reaction being positive, it becomes not merely negative, but destructive. Once rigor mortis has set in, there is no choice. The marriage is dead.

In most cases a relationship begins with romantic attraction. From the beginning, either the spark is there or it isn't. Even in a friendship there's attraction. As the relationship grows, it reaches out, illuminating the mind, body, and spirit. You enjoy your togetherness — doing and being with each other — and you share laughter as well as silence. When the time is ripe, you decide to make a permanent commitment.

How can either person guarantee that this glow will last? What are some of the clues to look for that will help us feel confident about the permanence of the relationship?

Marriage is the most serious, enduring choice of your life. When you choose to marry, you choose to *become* together; you undertake a quest to understand both yourself and your other half. What are some of the guidelines that can help you decide to marry, and to know you are making the right choice for you? How can you sort out some of the conflicting emotions you feel when you think about your loved one's past, which might in large part be unknown to you? How will you get along with a spouse's parents, grandparents, siblings, friends, children? How can you project how each of you, individually and as partners, will respond to the uncertainties of the future?

Before you choose to share your life with someone else, you have to know what you want to do with *your* life. Marriage doesn't have to be a trap. It can and should be fertile ground for two people to grow in love, self-respect, confidence, and awareness. Grace, joy, inner peace, and unity are possible only when one loves oneself and wants to share that. Nothing is more compelling than someone who enjoys life fully. That you're working intensely to achieve some exciting personal goal isn't dependent on the fact that you're alone or haven't met someone with whom you want to build a permanent relationship.

When you feel good about yourself, you care more about the physical and metaphysical world around you and the people who inhabit it. And it goes both ways: No one should live only for other people or solely for themselves.

One of the most frequent and worst mistakes in a marriage is to choose a companion because you find being alone too painful. Until we can embrace life fully on our own two feet, supporting ourselves financially as well as spiritually, we can't form or sustain an equal partnership with anyone. Before we can become *inter*dependent, we first must be *in*dependent. We must choose to work on ourselves before we decide to take on the inevitable challenges of marriage. We must be as whole and complete a person as we can be, so that when we take on the additional responsibility of a spouse, we don't have to give up any of our self-identity, but are enlarged by the love and support of our partner.

I could never choose to get married or to have children if it would require giving up my work. Anyone who loves her work yet thinks she can live without it might discover that life is hollow at the center in its absence. My interests and identity matter a great deal to me and cannot be sublimated through other people. In the symbiosis of marriage, each partner helps the other fulfill his or her own potential. You don't give up who you are or what you are when you

There is never a perfect choice but there are wise and wonderful and sensible choices.

marry; you take on other, additional responsibilities. You make the tough choices that Madeleine L'Engle spoke of at the Wellesley graduation: keeping all that you are intact, sharing and expanding each other.

Looking back, I see that I never had many role models of spouses who treated each other equally. Traditionally, it is women whose work is interrupted, as Margaret Mead's daughter Mary Catherine Bateson writes in *Composing a Life*. If a man was in the study working, the woman would go "shh-shh" to keep the household quiet. It was rare for the woman to be in the room with the door closed, the household shushed by the husband so *she* could concentrate.

By and large the pattern is now changing. We communicate differently. But the environment in which we were raised affects us deeply, and the influences often last a lifetime. Our roots, beliefs, customs, our decisions, quirks, predispositions, never can be completely overcome. A child can grow up to choose to do things differently from his or her parents and grandparents, but the mature individual who chooses to marry must be realistic; personality traits, attitudes, and one's capacity to love can never be completely altered. No marriage should be entered into as a kind of makeover plan for the other person. Your acceptance of and respect for the views and needs your partner feels to be important, but that are different from yours, will go a long way toward nurturing a growing exchange of love. Certainly one of the great liberating truths is that *we* can choose to change. If your father didn't treat his wife as an equal, you can choose to change this pattern.

Loving requires autonomy and is based on the ability to share one's self with another out of choice, as opposed to dependent need.

—AARON STERN

128

CHOOSING THE BEST

The choice to take on the commitment of a spouse is serious. Your spouse shares your bed, your bath, your free time. Your spouse's clothes are in the washing machine or on the bedroom floor. Your spouse has certain habits, needs, customs. You look at this other half. Will this person continue to make you laugh? Will this nice individual continue to be kind and good as a husband or wife? Do you trust the person completely? Do you feel you will be able to be a nurturer, providing the atmosphere to fulfill his or her needs? Do you want to grow old with this person? Are you swans who will mate for life? It's possible that you'll spend 200,000 hours with the person you marry, so the choice had better be good.

There are as many different kinds of marriages as there are couples. You choose both the person and the kind of life you will share. I know several high-powered professional couples who practically see each other only when they are out with other people, at events that will advance their careers. For some, marriage is little more than a mutual convenience, open in the sense that each person lives a separate life. But whenever we choose to commit ourselves to someone, no matter what the agreement, we should understand exactly what we're getting into.

Peter and I have been married long enough that I've

...the heart has its reasons which reason does not know.

—BLAISE PASCAL

Healthy couples choose to wait until they are more mature before they decide to get married. Traditionally, women gained the most security from a marriage in which the husband supported her financially, although this didn't necessarily provide women with the opportunity to develop their talents. Today women are bringing their education, their talent, and their own money to the table. When my father married my mother in Massachusetts in the early 1930s, he forbade her to work because it wasn't "proper" for a woman to receive pay. Even today there are men who have entrenched gender prejudices that don't always show up during the pre-wedding romantic stage. These biases usually surface when a couple settles into domestic patterns.

When I married Peter, I was living fully. I had a demanding professional career, I was raising two daughters, I was financially independent, and I had an attractive home decorated with antiques and art that I'd collected; my first book was being published in the fall. On a practical, basic level, I didn't *need* Peter. I was self-sufficient. But I was also a single parent, alone, and I wanted to share my life with someone I respected and loved.

I first met Peter when I was thirteen. I'd just won a tennis match; his older sister was my ladies' doubles partner. Peter was thirty-three, married and with three children. In the nineteen years from the time I first met Peter to the time we married, he divorced, remarried, inherited two stepchildren, had a son, and eventually divorced again. I married, had two children, and divorced. All this time we remained friends, seeing each other at social events, inviting each other to our parties. Few people have almost two decades to experience the personality of another person before they choose to marry. We did.

From the beginning, Peter was fascinated by my determination—first, as a circuit tennis player. His sister Barbara chose me as her partner because she likes to win her matches and so do I. Peter became interested in my design career, and believed it would blossom into something significant. He encouraged me when I began to write.

By the time we mutually decided to join our families, we knew quite a bit about each other. My ambitions were clear to Peter. His expectations were in line with my goals. After all these years, it is safe to say that I married a man of character, honorable in his dealings both private and professional. I've spent more time with Peter than anyone; Peter spends more time with me than anyone. This is a deliberate choice. We like being together. We're working partners. When we chose to marry, Peter decided he'd go on my book tour with me. Having a highly regarded trial lawyer carrying my tote bag as we went around the country together quickly made me realize that my career was intensely important to Peter as well. My self-expression brought him pleasure.

The first summer we were married, we rented a house on Orange Street in Nantucket and the place was bursting with children. Right away, we set up a writing room upstairs, where we wrote every morning until we all went to the beach for a picnic. We had fallen into the habit of giving each other gifts spontaneously and after a little time we realized that they reflected our commitment to each other's writing. Peter and I had bought each other antique inkwells; he gave me my first gold fountain pen. As wed-

Choices keep us up to date with reality and what we value as truth.

ding presents, we had each bought the other antique writing tables. Not only does Peter tolerate the time I spend working, he encourages it, and is proud of me. I love it when he's writing; I believe in his work as much as he does in mine, and I'm as proud of him as can be.

Your choice of a partner must encompass the potential of *being* as well as the desire to *be* an equal partner. From observation as well as reading dozens of books about marriage, I have found that this is rare. Peter isn't right for everyone any more than I am. But in marriage, you choose the best for yourself and *one* other person. You don't have to seek universal approval. Marriage is private.

I'm not embarrassed that I love my work. I feel the direct satisfactions from doing what I believe in and seeing the results. When Peter publishes a book, I can share his joy over the accomplishment too. A common feature of many marriages is that one person dominates the other. Until individuals have their *own* lives, they end up being a burden — emotionally or physically — to their partner. Only when two people work mutually toward individual and collective goals is real symbiosis possible. Peter feels comfortable becoming completely absorbed in his work because he knows that I am intensely involved in mine, and won't feel rejected while he is preoccupied with his.

Whenever one spouse sublimates his or her own interests and creative work for a spouse, resentment follows. Two people don't grow apart because each is excited about his or her own work and interested and curious about every aspect of it; people grow apart when they are unhappy, unfulfilled, and discouraged. If someone wakes up in the morning miserable, complaining about how awful

We are shaped and fashioned by what we love.

—JOHANN WOLFGANG VON GOETHE

life is, out of defense the spouse will play golf, go on business trips, have affairs, overdo it with alcohol or tobacco. No one likes to be around someone who is chronically unhappy; it makes it hard to celebrate the moment.

People choose to spend time together because it makes that time interesting and worthwhile. You must bring to the moment both your enthusiasms and your deeply felt disappointments. The fact that your lives are ultimately separate vitalizes the relationship. You have a good time together because you *both* contribute positive energy. You have independent work, but because of mutual respect and interests, you take great pleasure in the unfolding process. You do your part creating something together, each participating in whatever way is both natural and most useful.

In marriage as in lovemaking, each person feels separate sensations, satisfactions, and joys; the experience involves two partners giving pleasure to each other while simultaneously receiving it. When one person is pleased, he or she automatically brings enjoyment to the other; conversely, it causes pain to both when one spouse is dissatisfied for whatever reason. Two separate, equal partners, working together to create a life that is more dynamic, meaningful, and significant than a life alone—that is the commitment; and the commitment, not the marriage certificate, is key. The decision to stay together can never be enforced by a piece of paper. Vows are valid only when they are believed in and lived honestly.

Once you choose to marry, you also choose to make the adventure enjoyable or miserable. It's a question of attitude, focus, and expectation. If you and your spouse make an honest attempt to grow and find as much richness

Lovers never get
tired of each other,
because they are
always talking about
themselves.

—LA ROCHEFOUCAULD

✦

together as possible, caring and believing in each other, you will develop an understanding enhanced by mutual trust. The heartbreaking reality is that the person we trust sometimes violates that sacred confidence. Once there is a breach of promise, faith is lost and dreams are shattered. Adultery, for instance, is grounds for divorce in most states.

The maxim that it is easier to get into something than to get out of it holds true with marriage. "Until death do us part" is a solemn vow. We are meant to enter into a relationship that will color everything else in our lives and to remain faithful until death. This is the mandate. The reality of a 50 percent divorce rate illuminates the truth: The average marriage lasts just over nine years. Many young people today don't marry at all because they're afraid of making a false commitment. And divorce is *never* easy.

How complicated life can get when morality, sexuality, reputation, commitment, pleasure, pain, good, and bad are all inexorably mixed together! When a faithful spouse is suddenly unfaithful, everything is turned upside down. After *Living Beautifully Together* was published, a friend disagreed with my section on friends of the opposite sex precisely because of the danger of adultery: "Alexandra, you'd have to be an awfully strong person to have a close friend of the opposite sex." I smiled and answered, "When you're strong, you can have *great* friends of the opposite sex."

CHOOSING TO PART

If a marriage deteriorates and stagnates, ideally it can be terminated, and the two people are freed to begin to build a new life. While many times an indiscretion is regretted under these conditions, the regret always comes too late. When one spouse hurts the other, the violation of trust, confidence, and love changes everything. No one deserves to be betrayed; once a spouse has been unfaithful, the damage is done.

Tolerance and reasonableness might be a grace note, but each person in the relationship has the power to choose not to be a helpless victim. Once faith is lost, the relationship can *never* be the same. This is not a gender issue, something that women should be able to forgive in their men, but a true crisis that cannot be brushed off as a mere misdemeanor. I can't imagine a greater hurt than to be cheated on. If someone is unfaithful to you, what's your choice? Where do you draw the line? You may forgive someone, but you don't have to. What it comes down to is that if someone isn't serious with marriage vows, he or she isn't being serious with the marriage itself. "Until death do us part" also means "Until death *of trust* do us part." I believe we can always make the moral choice. A spouse has the power to uphold the dignity of another human being and the ability to destroy it. If a spouse finds he or she is attracted to someone outside the marriage, the right

If we deny or cover up anything that is at home in the soul, then we cannot be fully present to others.
—THOMAS MOORE

choice is not to consummate the attraction.

One of my favorite *McCall's* columns was entitled "Ingredients of a Happy Marriage." Solid commitment is the glue that keeps two people determined to communicate and work through problems. Mutual respect runs a close second. When you love someone, you don't want to hurt his or her feelings. We can't do anything, good or bad, without affecting our spouse. When we're supported by our partner in all our aspirations and we reciprocate that support, we grow closer together.

Two decent people who love each other, who want to support each other, should be able to grow to respect each other the more familiar their partner's character becomes. But what if you discover that the person you had high hopes for is really unstable and a disappointment? If you find yourself in a relationship with someone you've discovered to be self-destructive or destructive to you, what choices do you have? No spouse has the right to abuse and use another human being, psychologically or physically. Anyone who feels entitled to do so to you — in mind, body, or spirit — should be denied access to you.

Why do two people who start out so "lovey-dovey" end up hating each other? Does the role of husband or wife permit one to act in other than loving ways? Not everything about your spouse is going to be revealed right away. Like crimes, flaws often take time to be detected. When you catch your spouse doing something dishonest or cruel, how can you pretend you respect him or her? A marriage also can be faced with the fact that one of the partners is growing at a different rate than the other. In such cases the marriage can become something like a living death on every level—spiritual, emotional, and physical. From being lovers, husband and wife turn into strangers.

Personally, I've come to believe that a great deal of luck is involved when we choose our partner in marriage. There is no formula; the process is too complex. Good luck is a blessing when you're embarking on a lifetime partnership, but in the end, how well someone takes disappointment, how brave someone is during really tough times, is a mystery until the experiences are lived. When you commit yourselves to each other, you're implying that you will stick by each other no matter how dark the circumstances. But if you grow not to respect your spouse, for whatever reason, you have a choice. You can admit you made a mistake.

Marriage counselors encourage people to work harder at the relationship. Sex therapists suggest certain strategies, tips, tricks, and secrets. A lawyer is professionally obligated to try to get the married couple back together. There are certainly many instances in which relationships can be turned around through professional help. But when someone isn't right for you, for either basic or exceedingly complex and mysterious reasons, you can't force a reconciliation. The marriage could have deteriorated to such an extent that parting may be the only solution. If a couple chooses to stay together to share the mortgage payments, the food bill, the car—that's their choice, but marriages of convenience will never bring joy. The couple becomes locked into a dreary life of not-so-quiet desperation. When you consider that you only have so much time to experience the joy that can be shared by two people who deeply love and respect each other, you must choose wisely, even

All choices have great consequences.

139

if it means making the decision to divorce. Remember, divorce is always a positive choice — this is not to say that it is not *very* painful — because now you are both free to grow and open yourselves up to joy.

Peter and I don't work at our marriage. We never have; we work on ourselves. Because we love and respect each other, we communicate our needs. I try to be there for him when he needs me, in the same way that he tries to be there for me when I need him. We talk things out when we have conflicts, and together we agree on a compromise. I feel comfortable being myself in his presence; I'd rather have Peter with me than be alone. Peter is ideal for me because I'm attracted to him. He's not perfect, but the best choice for me. Because he is almost twenty years older, we tend to take less for granted than younger couples who feel they have limitless time.

We live with a sense of intensity balanced by serenity, peace, and joy amid vital activities. Each day is a fresh opportunity to celebrate our life together, our work, our families. We have fun just being together. We fuel each other. We share what we think and read, and we encourage each other in our writing. But it is not out of a sense of obligation or duty that we are together as often as we are. We live together, love, work, travel, entertain, decorate, cook, and garden together. We know this is rare. We know that many men and women don't like or don't want this degree of togetherness. But for us, it works. Our time together is *our* choice.

Of the blessings set before you, make your choice and be content.
—SAMUEL JOHNSON

MAKING CHOICES TOGETHER

Once we have chosen our other half, we should look at our expectations for the marriage and for our life together. Aim high. When you have hope, the marriage becomes a foundation of faith, a living mystery through whose grace you will experience transcendence. Believe in what you are building because the risks are worth everything. Break down gender roles and take a look at your lives at home. Who does the cooking? Who does the laundry? Who decides about the landscaping? Who picks the color of the living room? Who takes the children to school? The answer is that you work things out *together*. Everything mysteriously takes care of itself once you experience this new grace.

After making the commitment and sorting out your expectations, the third ingredient for unity that I believe essential is to choose to experience the adventure of life. Make a pledge together to spend a lifetime of learning and growth. When we're curious, we explore, try new things, see in new ways, take risks, and dare to live more vibrantly. Life is a process of growth; you can help each other in your quest for truth and have fun in the process of unfolding and becoming. Peter and I thrive when we're challenged. We like to try new experiences and are open to learning from everything around us. We love to travel, to do things, and this feeling of adventure arises from the

One choice leads
to another.

challenges and rewards of the choices we have made in our journey together.

If 50 percent of all marriages end in divorce, what choices can you make to avoid trouble? One study devised questions that can predict, with a high degree of accuracy, whether a marriage has a chance to last at least four years. Among the key areas covered in the questionnaire, according to *New York Times* health reporter Jane Brody, were:

- Affection toward the spouse.

- Negativity toward the spouse, which included vagueness about what attracted them to their spouse and how much they disagreed, and the negative feelings they expressed about each other.

- Expansiveness, or how expressive each partner was during the interview, for example, in giving details of the courtship.

- "We-ness" versus separateness, or how much the spouses saw themselves as part of a team as opposed to emphasizing their independence.

- Gender stereotypes, or how much like traditional men and women the spouses were in their emotional expressions and responses to their role in the family.

- Vitality, or intensity of their feelings toward each other when dealing with conflict.

- Chaos, a couple's feeling that they had little control over their own lives, or, put another way, a laissez-faire attitude that life is hard and must be accepted as such.

- ▣ Glorifying the struggle, or acknowledgement that there were hard times in the marriage, but pride at having gotten through them.

- ▣ Marital disappointment and disillusionment.

Among the couples who divorced, the husbands were likely to be "low in fondness, low in 'we-ness,' low in expansiveness, while also being high in negativity and marital disappointment," the researchers added. The report suggested that the husband's actions—specifically, a tendency to withdraw from argument—were most predictive of divorce. The tendency of husbands to stonewall was also found to be directly related to the development of health problems in their wives.

Spouses have choices they can make together. A strong, loving, lasting marriage is not created by chance but by choice. In her article, Brody concluded that "love needs to be fed—with shared experiences, joys and sorrows. This requires time, attention and emotional energy."

When you've cultivated your relationship by paying attention, spending whatever time it takes to nurture your life together, you will experience a closeness that seems to make you feel buoyant and alive. And when this bond evolves, you embrace all of life's inevitable challenges as two loving friends.

Only independent people can choose to remain in a relationship.... The most mature level of love exists only in the face of free choice.

—AARON STERN

▣

do; they are discouraged, and they wonder how they can take on the responsibility of having children of their own when they can hardly make ends meet now.

For Brooke, on the other hand, the question whether to have children or not has a clear-cut answer. She can't wait. The benefits so outweigh the drawbacks, in her opinion, that she will embrace the opportunity. She thinks that people tend to become self-centered when they don't have children. Yet Alexandra is looking forward to children as much as Brooke is, and both believe they can become good parents.

What are the factors that can help us decide whether or not to have children? If you have a career that requires your complete concentration and presence, like acting, perhaps you're concerned you can't be a good enough parent. Past generations jumped right in and had children without a second thought, but young people today are aware that they have choices. Many feel they're not ready. They're afraid; they don't want to give up their careers or they don't feel emotionally stable enough to assume responsibility for the well-being of another human being. Others feel that raising children in tough economic times would drastically lower their standard of living.

When a married couple decides to start a family, questions come up about how to raise the children. Do you intend to have more than one child? How will the child be cared for? What are the economics of educating a child today? Where is the best place to bring up a child? These are difficult questions, and conversations about them between spouses can get pretty heated. But the choice has to be made, and both parents must agree on it completely. If

The choice to have children is a lifelong commitment.

✦

a couple has a child when they're not ready, everyone loses.

Many couples today are choosing to have fewer children, or even just one. It's better to try to do a decent job with one child, they believe, than to take on more than they can manage economically and emotionally. The difference from previous generations is greater, too, in that women are no longer willing to assume the full workload of raising a child.

The woman who opts for the primary role in caring for a couple's children, who frees her spouse to concentrate on his career, has made a deliberate choice. I have respect for *any* decision as long as the person who makes it works it out fully and doesn't complain. In a society that pretends everyone can have it all, sacrifice is an unpopular, old-fashioned word. Yet sacrifices are always required to accomplish anything, and in terms of the bigger picture, they're always worth it.

A woman's choice to give up her own income and daily contact with her colleagues in order to care full-time for her family could result in one of the most rewarding experiences of her life. I myself chose not to stay at home full-time with my children. I'd seen the frustration this kind of sacrifice caused my mother. From quite a young age, I knew that I would try never to depend on a man for money. Having no chance of inheriting any, I had no choice but to earn a living myself. But that wasn't the sole reason I decided not to stay at home full-time. I *loved* my career. I especially enjoyed working with wonderful, talented, interesting women. I felt that by bringing my children into *my* world, I could show them how they *also* could

Only when choosing in freedom does the human being truly come to life.
—EKNATH EASWARAN

147

make the tough choice to continue with their careers and raise families.

I was enormously lucky. I loved being pregnant. I was young and fit. When I was preparing for natural childbirth, the woman instructor at the hospital said she rarely saw a woman who was in better physical condition. I was able to work a full day at the office the day before Alexandra was born. That evening I went grocery shopping, came home, ate a candlelit dinner of veal piccata, spinach, and a baked Idaho potato; I remember still being hungry just before going to sleep, so I had a toasted and buttered English muffin. Then my water broke. Within a few hours I was at Lenox Hill Hospital where, in the early morning, Alexandra was born. If it sounds like a fairy tale, it was. Still starved, I ate a breakfast of boiled eggs, toast, coffee, and grapefruit juice half an hour after she was born.

I chose to stay active the entire nine months I was pregnant. I was determined to watch my diet. I ate nutritious foods that would nurture the baby as well as keep me in good shape both during the pregnancy and afterward. I felt beautiful when I was pregnant. I loved feeling and experiencing the baby kicking inside my tummy. My happy experience was repeated with Brooke two and a half years later. I felt good, I exercised regularly, including playing in tennis tournaments. I chased up and down the stairs of the town house where I worked, as well as running up and down clients' stairs. For me, choosing to have my children when I was in my twenties proved to be a big plus.

I loved creating a nursery and anticipating playing with

Independence is the key to the capacity for choice.

—AARON STERN

my babies. To be part of the miracle of bringing forth another life was a powerful emotion. Once I was actually carrying a baby, I felt wonderful. I wore tent-style dresses, which were conveniently in fashion in the late sixties, so I felt stylish and rather special. I'm well aware how awful many women feel when they're pregnant. I'm also sympathetic to how painful it is when a woman has a miscarriage or when a couple loses a child to crib death or illness. I have friends who had to lie immobile in bed for as many as five months if they were to have any prayer of giving birth to a healthy child. There are never any guarantees. Bringing a child into this world requires being brave, courageous, and loving.

We bring a child into this world; whether the child will be a boy or girl is out of our control. We can, however, choose how we're going to bring up the child, what values and boundaries will be the backbone of the child's growth and nurturing. Everyone has to decide what is best for them. No situations are ever the same, no matter how similar they appear on the surface. The one constant truth, however, is that under normal circumstances it's not necessary for an active parent to become a full-time baby sitter at the expense of his or her own adult interests.

When Alexandra was being interviewed for nursery school, I guiltily confessed to the head of the school that I was a working mother. Mrs. Anderson laughed and replied, "Aren't we all, Alexandra. But don't worry—children don't break." My heart pounded. I felt *such* relief. Just as I couldn't give up my work for a spouse, I couldn't give up what I love to do for a child, either. Raising chil-

> He who does a good deed is instantly ennobled.
>
> —RALPH WALDO EMERSON

My fathering had always taken the form of a friendly cloud that floated across the lives of the children, and paused occasionally to cast a shadow. That they would turn out to have their own weather, and that I would profit by the climate, was an immense satisfaction.

—JOHN LEONARD

dren added a huge dimension to my already full life, but I didn't have to forsake my career in order to become a caring, loving mother.

As long as women have babies, by biological nature they will spend more time at home than their male counterparts. While they're home, they cook, decorate, garden, and generally set the tone for the family. Before making the choice to have children, a woman could have had a high-pressured career in the financial world, in advertising, publishing, or fashion—but once the children arrive she eventually has to choose how much she can juggle. Some women take a few years off in order to stay at home, focusing on their children's school, PTA, and charity work.

Many mothers who choose to stay home, however, end up spending too much time doing unpaid work—baking for the school, sewing costumes for the play, doing safety patrol three afternoons a week, and the list goes on and on. They don't have a moment's peace. They're home being full-time mothers by choice, but still they have to set limits. If a woman *chooses* to stay at home, she should also decide what it is she loves to do, something that is independent from her children, their school, their homework, her husband's success, the housework, the cooking.

Women have been going out into the workplace in greater numbers over the past forty years. There is a certain rush that comes with working among intelligent adults, networking with co-workers, choosing a career, moving up, earning increasingly good raises. But what woman, deep down, wouldn't admit how nice it would be to stay at home? Padding around in her bathrobe, sipping coffee, lingering over the paper, exercising to the aerobics program on television, bathing, tidying up the house, doing something fun with the children, picking up some fresh flowers, fruit, and vegetables, going to the library to check out some books, returning home, puttering about the house, listening to music, popping some wash in the machine, curling up with orange cinnamon tea and reading until the breadwinner comes home for a candlelit dinner. Ah, domestic bliss. Time to watch the children, to cultivate your own garden, to grow *and* smell your own roses. The career mother longs for a day in the week before Saturday when she can take the children to school after flipping eggs on the griddle, and have several productive hours to herself pursuing a secret dream she dares not discuss just quite yet.

But the stay-at-home mother doesn't decide to sip herbal tea from a china cup and saucer, listening to classical music, reading Chaucer. No, we can't make the choices we want every day. As mothers with careers, we will always experience awkward, agonizing times when we feel split in two. When we're drawn and quartered emotionally, we find it difficult to believe we've made the right choice. Our child is in an emergency situation. We can't reach our husband; he's on a plane. Our employer can't believe that Johnny is back in the hospital. Sympathy at the office is low. We feel like throwing up but we can't.

On the other hand, the choice to stay at home during the short, fleeting period in your life when you have pre-school children is a good one. That a woman chooses to stay at home, however, doesn't imply that she's doing nothing but mundane work at the expense of her own growth and fulfillment. Being home when little children are underfoot can be the most deeply touching and rewarding time in your life if you plan your time wisely. As Gail Sheehy reminds us, the delights of self-discovery are *always* available.

I've asked thousands of men and women about their work and children. The time in a couple's life that requires continual reevaluation and adjustment are the years when the children are young and need supervision. When I married Peter I moved out of my old apartment, which was a five-minute walk from my office, to an apartment thirty blocks north, which required more time traveling back and forth. I eventually went to the office only three days a week, working from home Mondays and Fridays.

I found this pattern enormously satisfying. Nearly two decades later, I discover that many career women are doing the same thing in order to keep up with their professional responsibilities and yet be at hand for their children. When I started my own business, I worked out of two renovated maid's rooms off the kitchen, which meant I was able to carry on professionally at home.

I chose, in effect, to bring children into *my* world, which was a pretty nice place. This decision is not for everyone and I'm sympathetic to different points of view, but I don't feel an adult has to make unnecessary sacrifices. As parents we provide a fertile soil for our children. But we aren't raising fragile hothouse flowers.

Because of your choice—to have a rich, fulfilling, financially rewarding career as well as raising children—you have to know for sure where your priorities lie. No one has to hang around the house indefinitely while their children are growing up. Spending time with a child, however,

Be not merely good, but be good for something.

—HENRY DAVID THOREAU

is a treat, a reward greater than any other, and time that can never be made up.

Perhaps the creative tension between loving being with my children and missing them when I was separated from them because of business intensified the joy of our times together. While I carried on doing what I believed was right for me, I was aware that I had two full-time jobs. I needed to be a good mother and I also wanted to create. I didn't choose the easy way, and I found the struggles challenging. My goals and lifestyle left me no time to be bored. And there was definitely an intensity, a spirit of ceremony, attached to everything we did together. We lit candles, we sang, we played, laughed, and cried. We had fun together.

If we approach daily events with excitement—if we are stimulated and stimulating—life becomes special, something to appreciate. An adult's discouragement rubs off on his or her children. If a parent is tired, frustrated, or tense, the child is affected. But, on the other hand, a smile is infectious. A mother infuses her personality into the children's consciousness because typically it is she who spends the most time with them. A reasonable attitude toward children is a choice too. Carl Jung believed that "it is enough to clear away all the obstacles that hinder expansion and ascent" when one is raising a child. He never recommended that an adult smother a child through meddling or a deliberate prying into the child's affairs. Parents bring children into their adult world; they don't revert to the child's.

My parents' goal, which they fell short of achieving,

was to raise their four children so they could go anywhere in the world and feel comfortable. When it was my turn, I wanted to produce well-rounded, happy children. Children are sacred and have a need to grow up, to go from birth to adolescence to maturity feeling good about themselves and the world around them. My job as a parent was thus to nurture the whole personality of my children. They were loved and therefore grew up to be capable of expressing love. I tried to teach them that you never win all the games, but that playing hard, doing your best, is more important than winning. Through everyday activities, I exposed them to ethical and spiritual values that would help them understand the constraints as well as the rewards the world has to offer.

I chose to nurture their innate creativity and curiosity so they could grow in self-awareness and confidence. I made a conscious choice to raise my girls differently from the way my parents raised us.

I believe my parents were too strict; they never allowed us to learn from our own mistakes, and their punishments were always swift and far too harsh for the crime. Some children don't need to be punished; punishing me, for example, was redundant because I was able to punish myself. In the same way, whenever Brooke messed up, she cried and went to her room. I didn't punish her; that she had disappointed herself was enough. When Brooke chose to come out of her room, she knew I'd be there ready to kiss and hug her. Nothing had to be said. It was felt. Not only did Brooke love me and not want to hurt or disappoint me, but she loved herself and didn't want to let herself down.

The acorn becomes an oak regardless of any choice, but man cannot realize his being except as he wills it in his encounters.

—ROLLO MAY

Alexandra and Brooke were God's gifts to me. I had no urge to change them. I chose to focus on and encourage their talents and creativity rather than constantly correcting their minor faults. I tried to keep things in perspective. Their rooms always looked as if a cyclone had hit them, but early on we made an agreement that their rooms were their space and not mine. They were never on display for my clients to see. Now my daughters have their own apartments, which look like decorator show houses. I'm glad that I didn't needlessly overreact to their normal adolescent messiness.

As Jung reminds us, "One looks back with appreciation to the brilliant teachers, but with gratitude to those who touched our human feelings. . . . Warmth is the vital element for the growing plant and for the soul of the child." A warm person has more of a chance of becoming a warm parent. It isn't put on or a deliberate effort; the warmth should come naturally.

As parents we must be whole people, fully living up to our potential in order to set an example for our children. Children need a certain amount of freedom to live their own life, to find their own character; parents must choose how to accommodate and healthily integrate children into their lives. Margaret Mead made it clear to her daughter Mary Catherine Bateson that her work came before her children. At the time this would have been shocking to most parents, but today Bateson is well rounded and well adjusted; she respects her mother's commitment to her work. It's not a bad message to any child when a parent is doing constructive work and making a contribution to society. Life calls us to independence. One of the best ways

We're capable of living up to our greatest human potential by accepting full responsibility for the choices we make.

As soon as man perceives himself as free and wishes to use his freedom, his activity is play.
—JEAN-PAUL SARTRE

to grow up is to choose to emulate an intelligent, hard-working adult. Daughters in particular need examples of women who live productive, successful lives.

Children have an uncanny ability to detect weakness, and so the healthy, fulfilled adult has a better chance as a parent or teacher to enlarge the child's unfolding potential. The more fallible we are, the more the child will inadvertently reflect our failings. By focusing on becoming a whole person herself, a parent can consciously avoid passing on deep emotional wounds. Being older than my children never made me feel in any way superior to them. I believed in the importance of their growth more than in my power as an authoritarian. They had to understand the world around them—including me—by first understanding themselves. A child conjures fantasies during this stretching and questioning period and it is essential to remain open and receptive, to listen.

Alexandra, for instance, daydreamed. Quietly but determinedly, I defended her from teachers who wanted her to concentrate on what they were teaching. But what Alexandra was doing, in fact, was turning the information around in her mind so it made sense to her. A child has to experience any parental message in action. The best teacher is someone who is patient, understanding, and sets a high moral, intellectual, and spiritual example. Parents can't teach if they don't practice what they preach. Children need to have adults they look up to, people who believe in their innate goodness.

Yet without many exceptions, parents seem untrained for the task of parenting. Most of us were really unprepared to be responsible for a child. We learned as we went.

We made awesome mistakes. But the biggest mistake a parent can make is to underestimate the greatness and potential of a child. Again, if we could treat our own children the way we wished our parents had treated us, we'd be doing a reasonably good job raising them.

Even well-meaning parents often fear the worst and tend to falsely accuse their children of wrongdoing. The ills of society, however, are not automatically reflected in our children. To assume without any real evidence that a child is guilty of the kinds of behavior that show up in statistics—anything from using drugs to being sexually overactive—is not only an error in judgment, but demonstrates a basic lack of faith.

It should be stressed once more that the worst error we can make as parents is to behave as though we were lily-white, that we ourselves never made any mistakes, and that what our child has done is reprehensible. Not only is this shortsighted, it is damaging to the child's self-esteem and dignity. We should try to be tolerant, to understand that in all but the worst cases a temporary setback is *not* a chronic behavioral pattern. The good news is that our children, just like us, can choose to change their behavior in order to get back on their path. Transformation of the spirit is within all of our grasps.

It is a selfish form of illusion for parents to attempt to protect their children from real-life blows. Overdefensiveness can paralyze growth in a child. If parents constantly cushion a child with coddling, car keys, and allowances, the child assumes he or she is special and immune; the parent is sending the child out onto high seas without a life jacket or knowing how to swim. Whenever money is

I have found the best way to give advice to your children is to find out what they want and then advise them to do it.

—HARRY S. TRUMAN

given too freely and indiscriminately, rather than being earned from labor or as a reward for excellence, the child learns only to lose resolve, discipline, and ambition.

Children need something far more important than the financial security of a trust fund. They need emotional, intellectual, and spiritual food. Whenever we delude ourselves that someone other than ourselves will take care of us, we become handicapped. Money that is not personally earned creates a false image, a false sense of security, and eventually a lack of self-esteem. I want my children to tap into their own essence and feel the wholeness that comes from believing in oneself and in what one does. Of course, this won't necessarily mean the highest-paying jobs. But whenever money is equated with power, status, and success, the wrong messages are being conveyed.

How can children live up to their parents' expectations and at the same time exercise their own will, daring to discover and become themselves? As the mother of adult children, all I can ever ask for is that they do what *they* choose to do with their lives. If they decide based on their own hearts, whatever they want to do will be the right path. When I mess up my own life, it's usually when I allow someone else to take charge of it. If something isn't already inside me, ready to bubble forth, it isn't right for me because it isn't authentic. The idea might be perfect for someone else, but if it isn't my truth, it isn't right for me. I stray from my path. With some minor exceptions, whenever *I* choose to do something, I enjoy the process. We all choose something because it is an expression of who we are.

BEING THERE

When my mother was dying of cancer, I spent a great portion of my time in Connecticut with her, a choice I will never regret. But whenever we focus on one thing entirely, we usually find ourselves neglecting other obligations. The girls didn't do that well in school the spring my mother died. I wasn't there to supervise them; I didn't have the strength to be attentive both places. After Mother's funeral, I was sitting alone looking out the window when Brooke, then thirteen, came over to me and burst into tears. "I feel fat," she wailed. We were expressing it differently, perhaps, but we were both grieving for something. I was grieving for Mother; Brooke was saying that she needed attention, that I hadn't been entirely there for her over the past few months. After all, Brooke certainly wasn't fat; by saying that, she was really saying "I feel sad." I understood she wanted a good hug, reassurance that she was loved completely, which is exactly what I needed too.

In reality, both my daughters' weight fluctuates, depending on many things, as mine did at their age (and still does). Gloria Steinem has said that "women are still valued more in the world at large by their looks than men are." In a revealing interview, she herself once confessed that the reason she wore her long hair parted in the middle was

All the troubles of man come from his not knowing how to sit still.

—BLAISE PASCAL

so she could cover up her "pudding cheeks."

Girls' self-esteem is so closely connected to their appearance that they are more likely to develop eating disorders than boys. Neither my daughters nor I have had anything but a healthy attitude toward food: We enjoy it and look forward to each meal. Still, the daughters of many of my clients and friends are anorexic or bulimic, and as I travel around the country I see that many women and children are literally starving themselves. Someone who is a natural size 10 or 12 diets and exercises herself down to a size 6 or 8. It's true that we feel good about ourselves when we aren't overweight, but being too thin is unattractive and imbalanced. What we learn once we mature is to select our hairstyle and clothes to flatter our face and body, not the other way around. Beyond finding your personal style and engaging in regular good grooming, excessive time and emphasis on the body is narcissistic and an emotional danger sign.

The best way for a child to perceive her body is to accept herself as a whole person—mind, body, and spirit. What is true and beautiful and loving inside always radiates outward. If a parent loves the whole child, the child feels self-worth and dignity. If a child is neglected or abandoned early on, as Steinem was, scars appear later in life. But a child is never doomed. Children can create their own lives and make their own way; in the final analysis, after the early formative years, the parent should *not* be necessary. Although separation and loss are never easy, they are essential. I would be flattered if Alexandra and Brooke felt sufficiently in touch with themselves to be content carrying on, raising their own children, and in turn teaching them

...the kind of person a human being becomes is determined in large part by the kind of activities he elects to emphasize.

—RENÉ DUBOS

160

to live *their* own lives. The sixteenth-century essayist Michel de Montaigne lived by the motto that he chose never to be a menace to himself or anyone else—good advice to parents raising children.

I never read "how-to" books about child-rearing. I just tried to do what I thought was right at the time; all the received theories, for instance that you shouldn't kiss your child too often, seemed foolish to me. We always took baths together when they were little. It was fun and easy. After my husband and I separated, I let both girls sleep in my bed. We needed one another. In every case I made choices based on the reality of our specific situation. I learned on the job.

I poignantly remember one episode. I was making the girls chicken salad sandwiches. I had garnished the pretty flowered plate, cut the crusts off the bread, and placed the four half-sandwiches in a pinwheel design. It was early spring. I had put a bunch of daffodils on the butcher block table in our breakfast room. The sun gleaming down on the intense yellow of the flowers made me smile. But as I placed the girls' sandwiches down on the table, I realized I hadn't made one for myself.

What was I thinking of? What was I going to do—nibble away at the leftover crusts while standing at the kitchen counter? I quickly brought their plates into the kitchen, added a sandwich of my own, and rearranged the wedges. A few minutes later, I called the girls to lunch. We sat down together, making a celebration of what had been a routine. From that day on, I made a point of sitting down with them, eating the same meal from the same china dishes. Brooke was three and Alexandra was almost six when this hap-

To err is human, to forgive divine.

—ALEXANDER POPE

The first few years of our marriage were rocky and turbulent. Although Peter and I have not had a difficult time building a strong, committed relationship to each other, the process of knitting our families together was difficult for me. I'm sure many couples have their greatest conflicts over the children—yours, mine, or ours. Peter's youngest son, Nathaniel, was suffering; his mother was in an irreversible coma, and he was devastated. I tried to be his mother, but he rejected me and rebelled against both Peter and me. After many confrontations, Peter and I had a serious talk. I was so discouraged one night that I wanted to pack a suitcase and take the girls to a hotel. I had had it. Peter told me to step back from the whole crisis. He told me he loved me, but that Nathaniel was *not* my responsibility. If he turned out badly, I wouldn't be blamed; if he turned out well, I wouldn't get the credit. Peter suggested I go about my life, doing the best I could, and ease up on trying to love and discipline his son. "Let *me* deal with Nathaniel," he said.

Easier said than done. My step-duties were far more onerous, I felt, than his. Women are by nature usually more nurturing, sustaining, and present than men, even the best of men. A woman still bears the brunt of every domestic burden, whereas the man escapes to the business world for much of the week. The man is not always aware of what's going on at home with his children, nor does he choose to face the facts when a crisis comes to the boil. All generalizations have their exceptions, of course, and Peter is the first to admit that he is sympathetic toward women who inherit the role of stepmother.

Traditionally, children live with their biological mother

I now realize that motivation and free will are more important than behavioral determination in shaping the course of human life....

—RENÉ DUBOS

❖

if the judge finds her to be reasonably fit — that is, not lying passed out on the kitchen floor. Judges favor the mother over the father in the case of divorce because she tends to be more compassionate and nurturing. Although in most stepparenting situations both biological parents take turns spending time with the child, Nathaniel was by necessity living full-time with his father. At the time, I chose to love and care for Peter's son, whom I'd known since his birth, and to mother him as I did my girls. I thought I could help him, but I was wrong. My efforts failed. One summer, when he was in his late teens and in a state of acute rebellion that was potentially damaging to our marriage and family life, I told him he could no longer live with us if he kept breaking the law and the rules of our household. He laughed in my face. When he got caught and I reminded him of the warning, he shouted, "You can't do this to me!" I quietly told him, "You did it to yourself." He took a train to Connecticut to live with his half-sister.

If you choose to marry someone who already has children, all you can do is make a sincere effort to be a constructive part of a stepchild's life. If you run into chronic resistance, choose to move away emotionally. You've done your best. Stepchildren are children, after all, and when they're starved for love, they often act in unloving ways. You can't force a stepchild to like you or approve of you or even respect and obey you. Remember, you didn't choose the stepchild; you chose his or her parent. By definition, stepchildren come from a "broken" home, and some have more difficulty accepting their situation than others. They have their past, much of which is unknown to you. There are loyalties to the absent mother or father that run deep. Nathaniel subconsciously resented me, which was understandable — I was in fine health, while his mother's life was over.

Remarrying someone with children is like getting a heart transplant. If you want to go on living, you wait for a donor who has a healthy heart that best matches yours. But, as we know, these transplants are tricky and not always successful. There's a great deal of resistance and ultimately a risk of rejection, but you have no choice other than taking whatever treatment you can. It may not feel right, but the fact is you don't have the authority of a biological parent.

You only have one life. If you can't be cheerful and reasonably happy in your own home, you have to make some tough decisions. Most children, including stepchildren, eventually outgrow the negative, self-destructive phase. I'm often asked if I would have married Peter if I'd known what I was getting into. Well, I would have thought things over more carefully, certainly, but I would have made the same choice to marry Peter because I love him. I had no choice about his children any more than he did about mine. Children are ours for life, for better or for worse. No matter how awful a situation becomes, no matter how bad the communication, one never gives up on a child.

It took time for Alexandra and Brooke to fully accept Peter. They had fun with him and adored him, but they also have a father they love. Peter chose never to try to play the role of father with my two daughters. He preferred to be a caring friend, paying attention to their needs, discussing situations with me privately. Alexandra and

Our choices tell
our story.

Brooke are the seventh and eighth children Peter has raised. When we joined forces, he was bemused. He had fun. The girls called him Peter Rabbit. He enjoyed living with the three Stoddard ladies, admitting that we have added great joy to his life. It was Brooke, after all, who proposed to him. When she was four she asked, "Why don't you come live with us, Peter Rabbit?" When he answered, "We should ask your mother what she thinks of the idea," Brooke confided to him, "I think she likes you."

Each person is unprecedented, unrepeatable and unique.
—RENÉ DUBOS

THE CHOICE IS OURS

Experts have spent lifetimes studying and gaining insights into ways to help nurture a child, but the verdict will never really be in. Every aspect of parenthood, from deciding to have children to figuring out how to raise them, will involve tough decisions. What values will you instill, and what standards will you set? How will you help your son to expand his boundaries, moving from dependence to self-sufficiency? How will you let go and free your daughter to move on her own, wherever her path may lead?

None of these choices is simple. There is nothing easy about being a child today, any more than there is about being a parent, but the choices are ours. Our immortality lies in our children. It's nice to believe that they will help find solutions for our struggling society, and to know that through them, long after we've gone, we'll still be playing a role in the mystery and miracle of life. Not a bad choice.

PART

THREE

7

BECOMING ONESELF

"I am no different from anyone else—except in
the choice of areas for the quest."
—ROLLO MAY

A STEP-BY-STEP CREATION

Throughout this book of choices I've discussed principles
and strategies for making tough decisions under difficult
and sometimes awkward circumstances. I've also discussed
our family—our parents, siblings, spouses, and children.
Now, each of us can face the hard decisions about how we
choose to live our *own* independent lives.

As the microbacteriologist and writer René Dubos believes, "we live according to certain principles which have
a human quality. This quality has emerged and continues
to emerge from the choices that we make throughout our
individual lives . . . that one remembers the past and is concerned about the future; that one manages to combine in
one's personal life such different attributes as rationality,

intuition, and feelings; that one can communicate with other human beings in such subtle ways as to identify oneself with their fate."

How many of us *really* identify with our own fate? If we're willing to make difficult decisions that define our character, decisions that come straight from the heart, and we're also willing to take responsibility for the consequences of our actions, we will discover that choice is what guides our personal destiny. The essayist Montaigne felt that our duty in life is to compose our own characters. Dr. Dubos believes that the shaping of our character can be our great, glorious masterpiece.

Parents, teachers, and mentors can try to hone our behavior, but what we do with our own lives is ultimately a personal choice. We choose to go on a quest for truth, believing that what we have to express matters, that what we feel in our own hearts must be acted upon, whatever the hardships or sacrifices. No effort to create something unique is ever as crushing as the decision not to create. Being true to yourself involves creativity. You are what you choose to become. Therefore your life and who you ultimately are is a step-by-step, choice-by-choice creation. The most miserable people are those who dwell on what might have been; "if only" is a curse. Likewise, there's always someone else to blame once we lose sight of the fact that it is *our* accountability that matters. Our parents *could* have encouraged us more; our spouse *could* be more helpful to us; our children *could* show more consideration; and so on.

Several years ago, Peter gave me an original edition of Emerson's selected essays, *Solitude and Society,* for my birthday. While I was touched by this leather-bound treasure,

Choose ourselves.
—JOHN BOWEN COBURN

at first I felt intimidated by it. It seemed too precious. I was accustomed to reading Emerson in paperbacks where I could make notes in the margins or underline favorite passages.

After admiring the book's beauty, I eventually decided to sit down and read it like any other. Most of the essays were new to me, so it proved to be an enormously rewarding experience. Words leaped off the pages like leaves falling from an oak tree in autumn. "I make my circumstance" and "Oh my friends, there are resources in us on which we have not drawn."

What is it that gives one person the courage to try the impossible, to be adventurous, to dare, to take risks, to create? The glory and burden of our lives is that we've been given the freedom to make choices, however horrendous. You can make mistakes, you can misjudge. But when you're free to choose, you face *hard* choices. When you're confronted with a roadblock, you're free to skirt around it. You quit or move on. My mother had a heart murmur that, her doctors said, would compel her to leave college and lead a quiet life. A family friend had a horse farm where my mother spent a great deal of time. It turned out she was a natural rider; heart murmur or not, she ended up jumping in Madison Square Garden and winning trophies. The rider and the horse work together to jump over the fence; more than a sport, it really becomes an art. But when the fence is raised so high that neither the horse nor the rider can cope, the contest becomes inappropriate, even dangerous. We can choose to push ourselves, but not *too* hard.

Alexandra and Brooke have gone skiing with their father regularly since they were little, and they have become very accomplished skiers. Peter and I went to Vermont with the girls for a long weekend, and naturally they wanted me to join them on the slopes. I hadn't skied in nearly ten years. While Peter used his intelligence and went cross-country skiing, I opted for showing off to my daughters. What a great skier *I* was! We took the lift to the top of the expert slope and, terrified, I schussed down the incline. I was the only one who knew just how out-of-control I was. There was absolutely no way I could have stopped, nor did I, until I crashed into the snack shop at the foot of the icy mountain. That combination of exhila-ration, madness, and accomplishment will, I hope, never be mine again. I put away my rented skis knowing full well that I had been out of control. I was lucky to survive unharmed.

The thing was, I *knew* better. My body wasn't in shape and I hadn't been on skis in years, but I was proud. Why didn't I take the beginner or at least the intermediate slope? Why did I have to go to the top of the mountain just because my daughters were? Sure, I was a natural athlete—they'd heard the stories. But this was madness. After my crash, I vowed I'd never tempt fate again.

When my mother jumped over those fences, she was one with her horse as well as herself. Mother gave her all to what she did. She was in charge, in control. Mother knew what she was doing when she went over those jumps. I was insane, thundering down an icy mountain in Ver-mont, in full view of my daughters—who would have been horrified if I'd hurt myself. I could have died, killed others, broken my neck.

Man . . . must be alone when he has to judge or to make decisions solely by the power of his reason.

—ERICH FROMM

Whatever we choose to do, we have to condition ourselves for the task. I have to admit, however, that since that ski incident I have repeated my juvenile reliving of the past with other sports. We were taking a family holiday once in Greece, in Corfu, on the Ionian Sea, when I decided to join Peter and his son waterskiing, something I loved to do as a teenager. The girls were eager to see Mom shine in the water and watched attentively from the beach as the boat picked up speed.

I was hopeless. I couldn't get up. Peter was determined to help me out on my next attempt. When his turn came, he used one ski, standing tall, waving to us on the beach. Eventually I was able to get up on my skis, but I was shaking, leaning too far forward, clinging rigidly to the rope. Peter took *lots* of pictures of those fleeting moments, which are in our family album, along with pictures of his son and Peter himself showing off. I'm mortified every time I look at them.

And then, a few years later, when Brooke was a senior in high school, I went to watch one of her basketball games. I was the first parent to arrive. Brooke and her teammates waved me down to the gym floor. One of the girls tossed me the ball. I stood in the center of the court, carefully lifted the ball over my head, and placed it in the back of my neck. As the giggling teenagers looked on, I launched it up in a high arc. It landed in the basket with a swoosh, not even touching the rim. There was much clapping and jumping. The girls ran to their coach yelling, "Did you see Mrs. Stoddard?" I quit while I was ahead. I hadn't held a basketball in well over thirty years, when I had been president of the athletic association in high school. That

There is no value in life except what you choose to place upon it, and no happiness in any place except what you bring to it yourself.
—HENRY DAVID THOREAU

one incident was fool's luck. In each case, however, I was resting on past laurels, wanting to impress my children.

By the time my daughters were born, I had switched my interests from sports to writing. Other than tennis and swimming, I'd given everything else up, dividing my time between family, home, and career. My choice to take up writing had not been a deliberate act, but a gradual realization that I felt exhilarated when I wrote. When I was young, I became a good athlete because I worked hard at every sport I chose. In a sense, I look at my writing the same way I used to look at tennis. To calmly stand on the court, stare at your opponent, serve an ace deep into their backhand court, then move to the other side and serve another ace, is an energizing sensation. Or bending so low that your knees touch the grass when you stroke a powerful cross-court backhand with enough topspin to put your opponent on the defensive, giving you a short lob you can smash with a crisp overhead.

Playing the game, winning, being on a team — we know how much of an impact sports had on our development. While I've been told that I'm a good athlete, I concentrated to develop my talent and skills. I don't regret getting up at six o'clock and riding my bike to the public court to see old Doc Marshall rolling the clay. He let me use his tennis balls to practice my serves until his first lesson at nine o'clock. Because he saw how much I loved tennis, he'd come over, take the racket out of my hand, and show me how I could improve my grip. "Here, look." He'd serve a few balls. "Try it, Sandie."

I'd go home in time to have breakfast with my brothers and sister. I'd wash, bleach, and spray-starch my tennis dresses. In those days we wore all white, including our Keds sneakers, which we polished with liquid that came in a bottle with a dabber on a wire attached to the cap. My gear was as important to me as my strokes. Eventually I stopped playing with anyone in my family because I felt they would hurt my game. I strove at tennis, which put me in a different league.

A SENSE OF JOY

Maybe it was those sunrise mornings at the public courts with old Doc Marshall that gave me the courage to keep trying and never give up. He would walk over to the other side of my court, reach into his baggy sharkskin tennis shorts, pull out a fistful of change, select a dime, and place it on the backhand tape of the service court. "See how many times you can hit the dime, Sandie." The bunch of change in his pocket rattled metallically as he moved around rolling and sweeping the red clay courts. He didn't set down a big half-dollar or a quarter or a nickel or even a penny, for that matter, but a puny, thin little dime.

Doc taught me that when you love something, you *play* it, you don't work it. I've felt that sense of joy in all the work I've chosen ever since. If I don't feel that sense of play, or fun, it isn't right for me; someone else, someone who had fun with it, could do it better. The work you produce should be satisfying. When you choose to create something original, you will inevitably feel joy.

All actions beyond the ordinary limits are subject to some sinister interpretation.

—MICHEL DE MONTAIGNE

A favorite lecture I give is entitled "How to Put Magic in Your Life Every Day." With two full slide carousels side by side, I show a combination of Impressionist paintings, gardens, architecture, house interiors, and details of foods and objects; I invite the audience to join me on a magical day, a day in which audience members can enjoy tea with a mentor, see a favorite art exhibit, fly to Paris to have lunch with a friend, write a love letter, arrange flowers, cook, give a dinner party, go dancing, sip champagne by the fire. In essence, they've experienced the perfect day. I show a Renoir painting of people doing laundry at the river's edge. One picture, by the wealthy art patron and artist Gustave Caillebotte, is of men on their hands and knees, scraping the floor. I comment that you don't have to love your work, but you have to love yourself while you work. Same chores, new attitude.

We can choose not to become brainwashed. We don't have to do what our parents, teachers, and spiritual leaders tell us is best for us if their advice in any way interferes with what we know is true for us. Everyone, all the "other" people in our life, think they know what choices are right for us. The truth is that those who try to help us may be well-meaning, but they could never make as wise a choice as we can, simply because they don't know us. When we, of our own free will, weigh our choices, consider the options believe in *our* ability to decide, and are willing to live with ourselves, keeping our dream alive and never giving up, we will experience joy. Neither my parents nor Doc Marshall chose for me to improve my tennis. Because it was *my* decision, I didn't consider it a discipline imposed

...everything comes to him who hustles while he waits.

—THOMAS EDISON

178

on me, but an opportunity to do something for myself that was fun and satisfying. I never felt pushed. It became fun to work to improve my skills.

THE PROCESS OF DOING

The world is in need of deeply committed individuals. As Eleanor Roosevelt suggested, "It's better to light a candle than to curse the darkness." Find work that challenges and stimulates you. Through your efforts to express yourself, you'll feel the pleasure, satisfaction, and joy of creativity. Being good at what you do, being accomplished, choosing to make necessary sacrifices in order to eventually become recognized as someone who has made a difference, is not automatic. The most critical thing is that you have these goals to work toward.

The people who seem the most unhappy are the ones whose time is taken up by too much that is repetitive, routine, and ultimately uncreative. If having a clean, neat house is a higher priority than starting a new project, life turns inward, and when that happens, self-pity becomes an insidious way of digging your own hole—and the deeper the hole, the less chance you'll ever escape. Complaining about your misery is self-destructive because it guarantees that you feel awful. I try to avoid what Peter and I jokingly call "icky-poo." When I see others feeling sorry for themselves, making excuses rather than courageous

Making choices is a creative act of self-expression.

choices, I see unhappiness. People who fill their time with unimaginative and boring chores lose their ability to enjoy spontaneity. It is only when we let go of our captivity to the mundane that we leave ourselves open to exhilarating serendipity.

Make a choice to begin working on some dream. Nothing will ever happen without your having the courage to begin. Of course, to take these risks means, as always, becoming vulnerable, making mistakes, even failing. But life can't be lived on the sidelines. The fun is challenging yourself to something you've always wanted to do. To do or not to do; to be or not to be.

The secret is that it is the process of doing, the act itself, that brings us joy. Even when I took the girls to the playground, I sat in the sandbox and made sand castles with them. I've never been a particularly good onlooker, not even when watching a good tennis game. I'd rather play. I'd rather *do*.

Years ago, I went to the ballet with a designer friend from the office. During the intermission, my friend laughed and said, "I love the ballet. It's so beautiful—the movements, the leaps, the grace, the costumes, the set, the colors. I've never had the slightest desire to be a ballerina. I'm glad it's *their* blood in *their* toe shoes." I laughed nervously and said, "It's amazing, the discipline it takes."

Sitting there in a comfortable velvet seat in Lincoln Center may turn into an out-of-the-body experience, but it isn't the same as performing, the touch of mystery when your entire being is riveted to rhythm and pattern. My mother enrolled my sister and me in ballet classes when we were growing up, although I was hardly an inspired ballerina. But once you've tried to do something, it helps you to appreciate what goes into it, like trying to paint a really good picture. Having studied ballet as a child helps me to appreciate good dance. If the dancer is totally absorbed and exhibits superior grace, one becomes aware that the performer is the one experiencing the greatest joy.

You might choose to cut back, eliminating unnecessary obligations in order to look for some free space for yourself and to pursue your deeper passions. We learn most about ourselves by how we feel when we do things; too much of our time is unnecessarily taken up by reacting.

Claude Monet once admitted, "I paint as birds sing. I don't want to die without having said all I've got to say, or at least trying to." That's a nice thought, a good choice, and something we should take to heart. I wasn't *born* a writer any more than I was born a public speaker. I gave my first lecture the same year my first book was published. Writing and lecturing are recent interests of mine, relatively speaking. All of us go through stages; that's how we grow. What are some things you've wanted to explore?

When I first started my own design firm, I helped one client with a large Park Avenue apartment renovation. I love seeing the results of knocking down walls in order to enlarge a space, making dark, cramped areas into rooms of gracious scale, with windows opening up to light and a view. My client was the president of a large chemical company; he also eventually hired me to do some corporate suites. John enjoyed my enthusiasm as I moved through the space, working with the architect and contractor. When we were alone for a few moments before a meeting one afternoon, John surprised me. "What will your next challenge be, Alexandra?" he asked. "You've been decorating and designing for a long time. You must have some thoughts about other things you'd like to do." How wise and prescient he was. Living your whole life on the same career track can indeed become repetitious; you take the safe, known road, saying the same things, designing in a particular style, eliminating the excitement of discovering something new and fresh.

I had begun writing intensively about interior design when John asked me that question, but within a few years, without my realizing that it was transforming, my focus tilted toward lifestyle and beauty. I was no longer writing *only* about design, but about the way the people I admire look at life. It wasn't exactly what I had set out to do when I started writing, but gradually I understood that it was, in fact, what I had to do; it was me.

In order to be ourselves, we look at the alternative situations, and then choose one that gives us freedom. Only in the adventure of growth, reform, and change, paradoxically, is true security to be found. And that quest, that adventure, goes on throughout our lives, intensifying as our time diminishes.

The art of no helps you to be clearheaded about what you believe is the right choice for you. I can't stress this enough. You have to be *really* tough-minded to make choices. The great mystery about choice is that because you will *never* be able to please everyone, nor even be understood by them, the only hope is for you to feel content about what you decide to do. I had always believed that I could combine both family and career; my choice was

When there is no wind, row.

—PORTUGUESE PROVERB

182

clearly not the choice for every mother, but I did what I believed was best for me.

When Peter fell in love with me, he gave me a gold chain made up of interlocking, hand-hammered circles, each link a little over an inch in diameter. To me, this necklace became a metaphor for how everything overlaps; a new beginning doesn't start from a tabula rasa, an empty slate, but from where you have been all your life. One experience fuels the next; if you're doing what you choose to do, you find that everything falls together in subtle, often miraculous ways.

> Follow not me,
> but you!
> —FRIEDRICH NIETZSCHE

❖

THE ART-SPIRIT

Creative people are always on the lookout for new things to try. When something is perfected, its creator becomes bored. After years of sellout shows, our friend the artist Joan Brady switched from watercolors to oils. She worked steadily for over three years until she felt comfortable with her new medium. Perseverance and tenacity coupled with ingrained discipline and an emphasis on achievement are major factors in keeping the creative spirit alive. You have to listen to yourself and do what your muse tells you. It's simple advice, but very difficult for many of us to follow. The key to our sense of well-being is to be guided by our heart, which yearns to choose the challenging, original path. Anyone who experiences the joy of flow as she creates must by nature spend a great deal of time meditating her vision.

We are going to be challenged all the time, no matter how we order our lives, formulate our goals, draw our conclusions, or make our choices. Many of us have chosen to stay at home with a young child and give up that second income, at least for a while. Some of us are able to make our home the center of our creative output. Many people are becoming increasingly fed up with the rat race and the cutthroat atmosphere of corporate life today, and we choose to be entrepreneurs, to make our homes our base. The computer and fax have radically changed the way people do business. Even people who need to be in a city, everyone from bond traders to literary agents to advertisers, are starting to work at home at least one day a week. The break from incessant interruptions at the office and relief from stressful commuting is refreshing.

When Mrs. Brown, my employer and mentor, was ninety-five, my friend Amanda Howard interviewed her for British *House & Garden*. When Amanda asked her how she was able to separate her professional from her private life, Mrs. Brown frowned, puzzled, raised her right hand, flicked it gently over her shoulder, and replied: "I've never had to. I've been *most* fortunate. Perhaps I've lived a charmed life."

At this point, my life is my own. All that I do reflects my passions and my loves. I envision my existence as a charmed circle consisting of three parts: half my time is spent on my writing, one quarter traveling—which includes lecturing and book tours—and the remaining quarter on business. Busyness. I would be a very unhappy person if busyness occupied a more prominent place in my circle. My private life is incorporated into this highly personal circle—not separate, but integrated. Who is it, what is it that holds us back from making our own choices? Choices that work for us, that make sense, choices that feel right because they *are* right. Why is it that we have a tendency to wait for others to decide for us, when in truth others can only take our freedom away from us?

I haven't regretted my own change of work habits for a minute. I work in the living room at my favorite table, or at a space in front of a big picture window in one office room, or in the front hall on a large French farm table, or in the library at an old oak refectory table, or at one of two writing tables in our bedroom, or on the generous expanses of bleached, sanded maple counters in the kitchen. But one of my favorite places to write remains my bed. Whatever works, works.

There is so little time we can call our own. Once I started my own business, I began seeing and experiencing time differently. It's well known that entrepreneurs work longer hours than employees, but when you can work at your own pace, pressing the buttons yourself, being in charge, in gear, you can accomplish more quality work, feel a greater sense of satisfaction, and experience the exhilaration of creative flow. I've learned that I'm more efficient when I'm able to work in a relaxed, attractive setting.

All of us work in some capacity. How many of us love what we do? How often are we in the flow?

There are times in our lives when we can't afford to have what we want. We all have rent to pay. But whenever

Whenever we choose, we live intentionally.

the choice is the materialistic over the art-spirit path, we're bound for disappointment. No matter how rich one becomes monetarily, enough is *never* enough. But sacrifice is not a pejorative term. If you choose to preserve your dreams, you can live in a continuous state of heightened awareness, a place untouched by the stressful, pressured rut of the fast track. I once met a man in Dallas at one of my adult education lectures. I asked him what he did for a living. "I'm a carpenter," he answered. His girlfriend hugged him and said, "Bruce is an artist, but because of the recession, he's earning a living building things." I admire that. I love that Bruce is working on a one-man show even though he doesn't have a gallery to represent him. He will. But he has to produce the body of work *before* he finds a gallery.

One of my editors loves to read and write; this has been true throughout her life. Now she prefers editing to writing, and she earns a living reading, acquiring, and editing books she believes in. She is doing exactly what she chooses to do; being paid to do it is almost a bonus. How many of us are fortunate enough to be paid for doing what we love to do?

My editor friend has the art-spirit. Her dedication, coupled with her great talent and judgment, add polish to everything she publishes. Quietly and steadfastly, she works on a book until it's the best it can be. The art-spirited person loves the work. The materialist loves getting the job done in order to get paid. Mrs. Brown's dictum, "Do a good job and the money follows," helps us to see that money can be a result of the art-spirit. But when money becomes the goal, greed, dishonesty, and inhuman-

Anyone who has got any pleasure at all should try to put something back.

—LAWRENCE DURRELL

ity almost invariably emerge. The person with the art-spirit is self-motivated and dedicated to excellence. While some exceedingly talented people are also artistically temperamental, they approach their work with a sense of personal pride because they chose to do what they do. Some people with the art-spirit work fast, as under a form of divine inspiration; others are more methodical. But all "go with the flow"—they listen and follow their muse, and, regardless of inevitable sacrifices, they are always determined to give everything to their work.

Not all of us are creative geniuses, but all of us are creative. If each of us chooses the art-spirit path, the universe becomes our playground as well as our farm. We are capable of tapping into the cosmic flow. Whatever you do, question if you feel your work is useful—to others, to you.

If you bring the art-spirit to everything you do, you will not only empower yourself, but you will help others to empower themselves. This attitude also reduces stress, allowing you to remain clearheaded about the importance of the day-to-day, the small, simple gestures and tasks we do, almost by second nature, that can be helpful to others. You can conduct yourself in a highly professional manner, for instance. A one-hour meeting should start on time, and conclude one hour later. By respecting other people's time commitments, you show that you respect, care for, and understand them. As a career woman, I have appreciated those highly professional men and women who understand that we all have limits.

When we're home, we can fuel our art-spirit in a variety of ways. We can paint, write, do carpentry and cabinet work, paint a house, raise a child; we can do needlework,

> ...You must know that I am entirely absorbed in my work....I want to succeed in expressing what I feel.
>
> —CLAUDE MONET

we can garden, decorate, cook, read, arrange flowers, play the piano; we can entertain ourselves and our family and friends. When you leave home to pursue your profession or career—as a surgeon, a lawyer, a minister, a teacher, a nurse, whatever—leave home with the art-spirit. Return home to the art-spirit. Let what you do at home and your avocation represent your higher self. A home that is lived in fully—where creative expression is released regularly, where you recognize your own passions and pursue them, where you regularly play—is a well-chosen home. Active participation, expressing yourself in *everything* you do, enjoying the rhythm of work and rest, puts your life on a balanced, satisfying plane.

Being away from home too much is a sign of imbalance. I become increasingly homesick if I'm away too long. On the other hand, if you cocoon at home, at the expense of not receiving stimulation from others, you lack essential equilibrium. Choose the balanced art-spirit. If you want to have children and still maintain your career, choose to have two children, not five. If you want to reduce stress, choose to live more simply, without giving up your goals. You'll find your time well lived. Your life will be a testament to courage when you make tough choices, but you'll have a lot of fun and success.

KNOWING YOUR LIFESTYLE

A very vital part of self-awareness is knowing how and where you really want to be living your life—in other words, your lifestyle. During the question-and-answer period at the end of a lecture in Lubbock, Texas, a woman asked me, "If you love nature and gardening so much, Mrs. Stoddard, it seems odd that you live in New York City. Why don't you live in a house with a lawn and garden?"

It is a bit odd, isn't it? Several years ago, in a bookstore in St. Louis, I met a woman whose enthusiasm for my books literally lit up her face when we met. She looked at me with radiant eyes and said, "You're my guru, Alexandra Stoddard." I was a bit taken aback at first, but the woman—Marilyn—was in fact a very warm and honest person who always said precisely what was on her mind. We became friends; a year later, when Marilyn was in New York, we had lunch together. We met at the twenty-sixth-floor office I was working out of at the time, whose panoramic view included the East River meandering around Manhattan and the landmark Empire State and Chrysler buildings.

Marilyn was surprised to see a gardenia tree dripping with blossoms as well as lots of daffodils in a vase on my desk. She'd been to offices in cities around the country, but not *mine*, and she was utterly delighted. After an elegant lunch at which we were joined by other friends, I

I only know there came to me . . . A sense of glad awakening.

—EDNA ST. VINCENT MILLAY

took Marilyn up to see the apartment. She'd never been in the home of a New Yorker. We got off the elevator on the sixth floor, entered our large hallway, and I flicked on the strong overhead lights. Her smile died when she walked across the living room and saw the high-rise buildings across the street. "I could never live in a city," she said. "I need trees and soil under my feet. How can you stand it? Don't you feel like you're in a cage? Don't you hate the noise and dirt? I'd go crazy in a week."

Marilyn was in the home of a lifestyle expert, author of *Living a Beautiful Life,* her "guru," but she couldn't imagine herself living in my apartment. Over the years I've heard a lot of compliments about our house, about the gardenlike atmosphere, the light, the sunny colors, the art collection, but never had I felt anything like Marilyn's misery. Yet I had to laugh with her. It *is* pretty funny when you view it from her perspective.

To choose a way of living that brings us contentment and pleasure—*that* is the goal. We choose where and how we live based on our expectations for our lives and the dreams we have for our children. But what's right at one time in our lives isn't necessarily appropriate later on. How many of us feel we made the best lifestyle choices? How well have we lived with our decisions? How many of us feel we have the freedom to make agreeable choices about where and how we should live?

When she was on her deathbed, my mother told me there was only one thing wrong with my life—I didn't have enough contact with nature. Mother was right. Since age sixteen, I've lived in New York City, in a series of apartment buildings, far away from grass, trees, the water, and

Just do your job
and let go!
—LAO-TZU

190

a garden. I've lived with more soot than soil under my fingernails. My mother knew, and now I do too: In many ways my life in New York isn't really me. But then again, how many of us can say we live *deliberately*, the way Henry David Thoreau suggests?

Have my nearly four decades in the big city been all wonderful? No. One morning years ago I was offered a ride back to the city from Westport, Connecticut, where I'd been visiting my parents. My friend's car was broken into in New York, and both my suitcases were stolen. That same year, one of my first in New York, I was mugged — the man put a gun to my head. But then again I was young and living in the big city. And, as Frank Sinatra's old song says if you can make it in New York, you can make it anywhere. While still in school I was able to land a modeling job that paid me $65 an hour, which was a lot of money in 1959. There were opportunities all around us. If they didn't mind standing in the back, students in those days could go free to the ballet, opera, or theater. All the museums were free. Everyone else at art school was poor too, but we were excited about our work, stimulated by everything around us, and felt an inner wealth and intensity that carried us through. After we graduated, we all did find good jobs. We felt empowered. We'd made it in New York City!

Because of the restless yearning to explore the world that my aunt instilled in me, I had *no* desire to settle into a house with a yard of my own. I enjoyed the convenience of apartment life with a doorman, a handyman, and everything I wanted, including good Chinese food, literally a phone call away.

We do not know where we are going but we are on our way.

—STEPHEN VINCENT BENÉT

New York has been good to me and good for me. I enjoyed raising the children here, where they've not only received a good education, but made friends with a wide range of people from different cultural backgrounds, which has made them more sensitive and understanding. They were challenged intellectually. Both Alexandra and Brooke like the city. But once they left for college, it lost its glow for me. The apartment was no longer home. It became a series of rooms more often empty than not. Peter and I were mugged in front of our apartment several years ago, and ever since we've felt less safe walking the streets, even in daylight, in our own neighborhood. The city where Peter had lived since he was five no longer felt safe.

When you mature, security matters more. Since we bought our cottage in Connecticut, our focus has shifted away from New York. We now go to the country to live; we escape the city as soon as we finish our work.

When the legendary decorator Billy Baldwin retired, he left New York; he told friends that the only way he could enjoy the city fully was when he was actively working. It's true—there's so much noise, dirt, and bustle that the notion of *being* instead of *doing* seems incongruous in a contemporary urban area. I now prefer to work hard and leave.

My mother would love to see me riding my mountain bike around our village, sitting on rocks at the point to watch the sunset, digging in the soil again after all these years. Since the day I moved to New York, my mother never saw me dirty. I was always in my working clothes, which meant a dress or suit.

Our choice about where to live has to fit our means of

He lives to express himself, and in so doing, enriches the world.

—HENRY MILLER

192

making a living. But at any point in our lives we can make choices that are sensible for us. The most important thing in making a decorating choice also applies to lifestyle. Mrs. Brown taught the designers who worked for her that when you change one thing, you have to rethink *everything*. What have you always wanted to do but have been awaiting the right time for?

8
FRIENDS AND SOCIAL LIFE

There is no hope of joy except in
human relations.

—ANTOINE DE SAINT-EXUPÉRY

FRIENDS

When we choose to become who we are, we learn to know whom we want as our friends. And friends are no more automatic than any other part of our lives—we choose them. "Have no friends who are not as good as yourself," Confucius advised us.

The word "friend," like "love," is tossed around too freely. A real friendship develops into a responsibility, a loyalty toward the other person. It is possible to have only a limited number of friends, and we must choose them wisely.

What are the qualities you choose in a friend? What do you wish to share? I value trust above everything else in my friendships; if I trust someone, I am free to be my-

195

self. And the trust must be mutual. The key to abiding friendships is reciprocity.

There are a handful of friends I hold in the highest regard and care about dearly. These men, women, and children from all over the world are indispensable to my happiness. Authentic friends are not fair-weather friends; the bond is deeper. Friends teach us how to be compassionate, and they also let us show our appreciation for what we value most in our lives. When we really trust, respect, and care about one another, we choose to help and encourage our friends in *their* quests, no matter what they may be.

There is a big difference between friends and acquaintances. When a friend needs us, we choose to be there for them. We've all been through some tough times with our friends, but we stick by them out of loyalty and love. When we're there for each other in spirit, through thick *and* thin, we broaden ourselves, experiencing the enormous range of life's possibilities as well as stretching our own potential. When I wrote about friends in *Living Beautifully Together*, I suggested that it's rare for two people to grow at the same pace throughout life. If you discover that you no longer look up to a friend, that you've come to value different things, you choose to move on, making room for a new friendship. You don't have to have a formal break; you can be nice and kind about it, but you simply pull back. Real friends should uplift us, sustain us, make us laugh, help us to accept the truth, and bring us joy. When someone wants something from us that we're unwilling to give, something that in any way compromises us, we have to stand up for what we believe is right.

When I wrote about friends, perhaps I'd been living a

Friendship is almost always the union of a part of one mind with a part of another; people are friends in spots.

—GEORGE SANTAYANA

charmed life: I suggested that when you outgrew a friend and chose to make room for someone new to enter your life, you never needed to make a clean break. I've reconsidered a bit now. If someone you consider a friend is disloyal, dishonest, deceitful, or has developed the wrong values, a clean break is best—the person in question, you come to realize, wasn't really a friend in the first place. Once you've lost respect for someone, you can let go, walk away without guilt.

Business acquaintances are different, but the people we meet through work sometimes turn into real friends. Some of the people I value the most in my life are colleagues. We don't choose these friendships as much as they are chosen *for* us, but professional relationships can flower into extremely close bonds of mutual respect and affection. People advise you not to mix business with friends; while I understand the risks involved, I disagree. I have faith in the people I'm doing business with, and I believe that they will be fair in their dealings. The same rules of decency apply when the friendship is professional as when it is not. If the right ingredients are there, the development of a business relationship into a friendship can be a profoundly satisfying event. But if there is even a hint of exploitation, the financial connection is the rock upon which a friendship usually founders.

Friends don't abuse a relationship. Friends don't take advantage of each other. Everyone, for instance, has to earn a living. Asking for favors from friends is acceptable, up to a point—what friend won't give a little free advice here and there? We're usually flattered when someone asks to pick our brains, because it implies we know something

Choose to support
the aspirations
of others.

197

that can be useful. We all do favors for our friends, but we shouldn't be cajoled into situations where we are manipulated to the point of feeling uncomfortable. Be clear-headed about where you draw the line. Exercise your no. If you do, you won't suffer from regret or guilt later on.

Friendship isn't an open invitation to impose on or take advantage of another person. Some of my closest friends have never asked one favor of me. All they wish from me is that I *be* myself and continue to grow and develop. These real friends care how *I* feel. If friends were to ask something of me, they would also have to honor my no. You won't lose a real friend by choosing to set boundaries; you're always better off doing what you believe is right. Be cautious when seeking free advice and services from a friend, and never use your friendship as a financial shield. The reason business friendships work out is because it's implicitly understood that the friendship won't cloud the professional relationship. You can't hire a lawyer and, because of your friendship, not pay him. By definition, friends never want to harm their friends. Better err on the cautious side; friends are much harder to come by than money.

Whenever you have the slightest feeling that you may be imposing on a friend, talk about it. Discuss things frankly as you go along. By listening to what he or she says, you can always tell if you're pushing a friend too hard. What goes for money goes for time. A friend might want to be with you when what you really need is some time alone. If you don't have private time in which to center your mind, you're doomed to merely going through the motions. Emotionally you're a million miles away. Sometimes you just have to choose what's best for you.

No matter how subtle they are, the signals are always there. You and your friend are not a unit; you're not married to each other. You're friends, two independent people living individual lives. What one needs doesn't always coincide with what's best for the other. Sometimes, no matter how inconvenient it is for you, you must simply drop everything and succor a friend in need. Sacrifice is a choice we will often make for our close friends.

It isn't the role of true friends to reform or make each other over. Good friends have fun when they're together, have enormous respect for each other, and understand how precious each time they spend together is. They know they don't have to see each other on a strictly scheduled basis. All of us have limited amounts of time, money, and energy. I know that I'm not often able to spend as much time as I want with the friends I love the most, but I also know that any number of quick lunches or brief half-hour visits isn't the answer. We're friends, and we're more than willing to wait until the times when we can spend long, leisurely hours together under the best of conditions.

A friend of mine's advice about friends was "The greatest gift you can ever give to someone else is to never be a burden to them." This can be a worthy goal, but we all fall short of it because of genuine needs. When a friend of ours is in a serious crisis and needs to talk, the fact that we can just be there, listening, makes a real difference. Though we might not have said a word, we know that our presence counted. We didn't do anything other than listen lovingly; we gave dignity by not judging but simply being there, listening. Friends will be there for us the way we

Forget injuries, never forget kindnesses.
—CONFUCIUS

are there for them. But if a friendship becomes a litany of things negative, you can choose how to respond. No one can take advantage of you regularly without your choosing to let them. Take little steps to redirect the relationship. Gently interject your point of view. Respect the other person's feelings even if they don't exactly coincide with yours; always say what you feel is right, but pick the moment carefully.

Orson Welles was once quoted as saying somewhat cynically, "When you're down and out, something always turns up—usually your friends' noses." While some friends are always genuinely concerned about you and always care, there are the others who are not rainy-day companions. But only those who enjoy celebrating the good times and who also choose to be there for us during the sorrowful times are our real friends. Emerson reminds us in one *Courage* essay: "In the most private life, difficult duty is never far off." There are many times when we're down and out and need to be with a friend. If you're fortunate, your friend will recognize your needs with sympathy and understanding, not pity.

The misery-lover might be attentive, but is certainly not constructive to have around when you need cheering up. Despondency doesn't need encouragement. And the best kind of friend to have around when you're experiencing pain or sadness is someone who understands the value of gentle laughter.

At a conference in Cannes, Peter and I met a fascinating man, Misuo Aoki. When he isn't lecturing and teaching around the world, Aoki works with dying patients in Hawaii. A wise, gentle, and affectionate man, Aoki is more

But friendship is precious, not only in the shade, but in the sunshine of life....

—THOMAS JEFFERSON

than aware of how healing the right word at the right time can be. He didn't lose sight of this fact when he himself was in a crisis.

When Misuo Aoki had open-heart surgery, his friends gathered around, feeling sorry for him and interfering with his recovery. At a certain point, the truckloads of sympathy, though nice, became a bit too much. He couldn't stand it any longer; his friends were making him feel worse. When the phone rang with yet another condolence call, he answered: "Wait a minute. I'm seventy-seven. At my age I feel entitled to have my heart opened up."

It was Misuo Aoki who recommended that I read the philosopher Martin Buber's *I and Thou,* which illustrates that we become who we are because of our relationship with each other. Grace is possible only in an I-Thou encounter. Accepting each other can be an awesomely powerful experience. You dare to listen, sharing each other; there are no limits. You are transformed. How amazing it is when friends look at each other without looking away. Buber writes, "Only as the you becomes present does presence come into being. . . . The actual and fulfilled present exists only insofar as presentness, encounter, and relation exists."

Friends. I and Thou. This is serious. When friends are present for each other, each can receive the gift of grace, a gift I want to share with my friends until the last celebration.

Society exists by chemical affinity and not otherwise.

—RALPH WALDO EMERSON

SOCIAL LIFE

"Put any company of people together with freedom for conversation, and a rapid self-distribution takes place, into sets and pairs," Emerson noted. "They separate as oil from water, as children from old people, without love or hatred in the matter, each seeking his like; and any interference with the affinities would produce constraint and suffocation. . . . Leave them to seek their own mates, and they will be as merry as sparrows."

Why is it that we tend to see our friends one-on-one, enjoying time alone rather than seeing them in a social setting? It never fails: If I'm at a reception or party and catch a glimpse of friends, like a magnet I'll move through the crowd toward them.

But it's also true that the wider your net, the greater the opportunity to meet like-spirited people. In *Living Beautifully Together,* I wrote that at any moment you could meet someone who will profoundly change your life. When Peter's mother first started seeing her companion, thirty years after the death of her husband, George Brown, her friends would ask her where they had met. Peter's mother would smile and say, "A concert." Years later her companion, Walter, confessed that they met on a park bench in New York's Central Park, near the 72nd Street boat pond.

Moving around, attending social events, increases our opportunities for enriching our lives. Be flexible. You

It is prudent to pour the oil of delicate politeness on the machinery of friendship.

—COLETTE

could join a book club or sign up for a writer's conference. Whether you choose to go to a church supper, a folk dance, a craft fair, a Zen retreat, or a benefit dinner, search around for opportunities that will interest you. Sign up for a dance class or show up at an autograph party at a bookstore. Go to a school reunion or arrange to get all the cousins together for a picnic. Go to the preview party of an antiques show.

It is a basic human need to participate in stimulating activities with interesting people. Be clear-minded about your intentions to participate. Until we choose the course our own life should take, we will waste precious time. Someone once said, "What a shame it is to find out at the end of life what's so important." We learn about our needs through experience, trying out different kinds of activities and a variety of different associations.

Your life is spent with family, friends, at church, or temple, at work, at charitable or sports events. How do you choose what to do and what not to do? (Although always keeping in mind that just because you *can* doesn't mean you should.) Many of us have a certain number of social obligations in which we have no choice but to participate—a friend's wedding, a business dinner, a funeral, a favorite charity's benefit evening. But often we can choose to attend events where we are not involved emotionally, where chances are we won't know many people; we can go to a lecture or a seminar that will stimulate, even inspire us. And we'll generally meet *someone.*

Do you, like me, differentiate between your friends and your social friends? When I think of friends, I envision active participation in their lives; I envision a total commitment. Social events are a little more diffuse. The essayist Logan Pearsall Smith believed, "We need two kinds of acquaintances, one to complain to while we boast to the other." It's theater in the round. Social life is image-related whereas friendship isn't.

One of the obvious differences between friends and social acquaintances is scale. We only have the capacity, René Dubos writes, to be really close to approximately twelve people. We have limits. We go to a huge event and unless people wear tags we can't remember their names.

When I submitted my first draft of *Living Beautifully Together*, I began my "Friends" chapter by admitting that my best friends are my family: Peter, Alexandra, and Brooke. This was edited out—I was meant to be writing about non-family relationships. But I have to admit that I do put my family first. Peter, Alexandra, and Brooke *are* my best friends. I'm closer to them than to anyone else on earth. No matter how scattered we are geographically, we manage to communicate by letter, cards, and telephone. As a result, a great deal of our social life revolves around the fact that we choose to be together.

As a family, we've always enjoyed the art of dinner-table socializing. Good conversation, food, fun, and laughter sustain us. Our friend Marsha Mason and Peter and I met in Paris the summer Brooke was studying there. We took turns treating Brooke and her friends to glamorous lunches, including one in the garden of the Ritz Hotel. We'd get dressed up and have moments as big as years; we couldn't have enjoyed ourselves more. Peter and I also share our friends with our children. When the girls were

Every man has a history worth knowing, if he could tell it, or if we could draw it from him.

—RALPH WALDO EMERSON

young, they were always included in our parties instead of being sent off to their bedrooms.

When we're all together, with our close friends and theirs, there is no guile. Everyone is thrilled to be there; there's nothing intimidating, no uncomfortable feelings. Everyone is accepted just as they are. We embrace one another's differences. Inevitably we create an atmosphere of mutual affection and admiration. Families *can* do that, but friends always do.

Peter and I enjoy our social life, but as much as possible we keep it mostly to New York. When we go to Connecticut, we choose to be quiet. But wherever we are, we prefer small lunch and dinner parties where real conversation is possible. It's nice to be able to listen to and *hear* other people.

Each of us should watch our social activities carefully. Choose to keep a balance; too much social life can leave you feeling spent, and too little isolates you. If you go to a huge party you'll often end up seated with strangers, and in the noise and excitement it's next to impossible to have a meaningful conversation with someone you don't know. You end up forcing a smile and leaving early. It's undeniably better when the group is smaller and more intimate. We enjoy having a reception for our artist friend when he's giving a show of his work; it's fun having parties for friends of the children who have started a theater group. We like to go to gallery openings, botanical garden spring festivals, and the village Fourth of July celebration. Each event we may want to go to has its special circumstances, but when you review your priorities, you realize that you

Bitter or sweet, we don't want any part of life to be really over; it should always be available, if only through people who have shared it. When they go, they take a part of you with them.... But the roots remain. The roots that will forever keep calling you back, begging, "Come home."

—MARJORIE HOLMES

At fifty, you can look forward to coming into your own and you have earned the right to choose. You know what will sustain you and what your needs are. You let yourself be guided by your instincts, because your instincts are grounded in experience. William James assures us: "Wherever a process of life communicates an eagerness to him who lives it, there the life becomes significant."

Making an art out of living is for us to choose. Our experiences have allowed us to reach some conclusions about the choices that have been helpful to us. We've learned that we *can* control our feelings to a far larger degree than we ever thought possible. We've also come to know that our thoughts, the beauty or ugliness in our environment, the unity or chaos in our immediate midst, the people with whom we associate, make a big difference in the quality of our lives. I'm willing to make whatever choices are necessary in order to live this second half of life on my own terms, exercising freedom in a responsible way. I fully understand that I am and always will be free, and that I can choose to whom I will be accountable.

When I turned fifty, Alexandra turned twenty-five; she was entering the first stages of adulthood while I was crossing the threshold of a new half-century. In many ways she felt my age and to a degree, I felt hers. She felt more weight on her shoulders than I have felt on mine. Here Bob Dylan's words are apropos when he says that we become younger—lighter in spirit—as we mature. As you get older, you become wiser and less serious. You learn to give a polish to your sense of humor every morning when you get up, and you realize that many things that you thought were so important really aren't.

Our only choice is how we will face the inevitable changes which come to us.

—ARDIS WHITMAN

Alexandra's work paid just about as much as unskilled labor and she experienced very much the injustices that often go with being a female and young in the work force. She had no boyfriend. In an earlier generation, at her age, I was married, had a career, and was pregnant with the first of my children. Often, she has remarked, "Mom, I don't know how you did it."

My choice of interior design as a career proved to be a good decision and for a number of years life bounced along quite agreeably. Then came my divorce. The choice to separate was a painful one and the self-righteous disapproval of some friends was hard to bear. I learned that there *is* a truth inside us and that we can derive strength from that knowledge.

Scott Peck is courageous and correct in stating in the opening of *The Road Less Traveled* that life *is* difficult. But what I understand now is that it's not the struggles and crises that rob us of our vitality, but rather our lack of courage to face the truth. Someone once told me, "You can't go on repeating the same thing and expect a different result." To live the heights and depths of a full life in which we love, suffer pain and loss, and are brave enough to make changes, is always a choice.

Tough choices require trust from us—a conviction that no matter what awaits us at the other end, it will be bearable and we will be able to deal with whatever comes our way. We will never arrive at a destination that is either totally safe or *completely* satisfying, but we can seize opportunities for action, for choice, no matter how risky the options may seem. The people who inspire us to live on a deeper level of consciousness are those who are brave

We cannot cure the world of sorrows, but we can choose to live in joy.
—JOSEPH CAMPBELL

enough to face *their* challenges. Between the non-choice of birth and the non-choice of death, we should concentrate on the best choices we have in the time that is ours.

Death gives us a deadline. When you're told you're dying, you have no time to procrastinate or live for the future. A dying person, out of necessity, can only seize the beauty of the moment. Suddenly, living and all its potential is in perspective. The choice is to enjoy what you have left. Some unmet needs can be cared for, some problems solved, and some affairs put in order. Don't wait until you're told you have a short while to live; choose life in the full awareness that you will die. Therefore, keep your affairs in order, pursue your favorite work now, love your family now, go on that trip, see that friend, make that phone call. In other words, choose to live abundantly today.

Struggle and suffering are at times unavoidable but they shouldn't turn people away from life; rather, the focus should be shifted to what and who can be loved and appreciated. Whenever we awaken to a new day, we can *choose* to feel grateful for life, and breathe in all its riches and beauty. Or we can decide it's not worth the effort — there's no hope; living is too difficult. Many people, unfortunately, prefer to be told how to live rather than choosing to exercise their free will.

People who live inspiring lives encourage us all. People who live as though they'll be around forever, but with the vibrancy of someone who will die before sunset, are often our greatest examples. Albert Einstein believed: "The most beautiful thing to be felt by man is the mysterious side of life. The mystery is that we choose life in the certainty of death. We live one day which can fill us with such joy we

I don't want to die without having said all I've got to say, or at least trying to.

—CLAUDE MONET

feel a renewed passion to live as well as we can. The passionate are always our best teachers."

What makes certain people seize life? Why are some people open to growth, to unfolding, to deepening and broadening? Some people do have an enormous capacity for maintaining a steady equilibrium, for accepting what they cannot change, for facing what they can, and moving on. What do *we* need to empower ourselves, to be independent and free?

A life is self-created and it requires effort. When we face struggles and losses, we can choose to make the changes that will be best for us. We can choose to embrace both the rain and the sunshine.

View your sensitivity as your strength, your vulnerability as your wisdom. Be humble but not self-effacing. Struggle to bring forth all that is of deep meaning to you and express these feelings; share your insights with others.

LETTING ART INTO YOUR LIFE

The way I've come to look at life now, at the noontide of my own journey, first started becoming clear to me from a couple of incidental encounters that took place some thirty years ago. In 1959, the contemporary French artist Nicholas de Staal had a retrospective exhibition at the Guggenheim Museum. From the moment I saw them, De Staal's pictures haunted me, and I returned to look at them many times before the show closed. It wasn't until two years later that I came across Roger Muhl, another artist who had an equally powerful impact on me. I was working for a decorator, Jane Christian, who suggested that I go see this artist's first show in America because a client in New Orleans might be interested in some of these paintings for her house.

As soon as I walked into the gallery, I felt a visceral response: Muhl was painting for *me*. I became so intensely emotionally involved that momentarily I forgot our client in New Orleans. I walked around as if in a trance — one of those extraordinary times when you lose yourself completely in someone else's work.

What was going on? Why was I reacting like that? Certainly, I could not afford to own one of these pictures, but perhaps our client could hang one over her mantel — but, I wondered, would she ever feel the way I did about Muhl's work? I may have been in the gallery an hour or a whole day, I don't know, because I lost all sense of time and space. When the gallery owner came up to me commenting, "Aren't they beautiful?" I was jolted back into the here and now, almost upset to have the spell broken, but relieved at the thought that there was someone who could understand and perhaps share my reaction. When I turned away from the painting to greet the man before me, tears welled up in my eyes.

I had to run or I'd be late for lunch with my mother. But I had no appetite for anything except these pictures. After lunch we walked back to the gallery so she could have a look. Mother and I had been going to museums ever since I could toddle, but this was the first time I'd expressed a passion for a contemporary painter outside a

Choices intervene also in esthetic questions....

—RENÉ DUBOS

museum setting. Seeing the canvases again only reinforced my feelings. They touched my soul. As I stood spellbound before a cool snow scene, Mother punctured the silence, saying: "I've always intended to buy you an original work of art and I have been waiting for the right moment. Darling, is this a picture you'd want to live with forever?"

I couldn't believe my ears; the whole day was so unreal. Happily I accepted my mother's largesse, though it involved a real financial sacrifice for her. The painting cost a fraction of the price of a Nicholas de Staal, but it was still a lot of money. When I returned to the office, Miss Christian was pleased that I was so enthusiastic about the exhibition. I sent our client some photographs of the paintings, and she selected one on approval, which she ended up keeping. My snow scene hung over our living room sofa; it continues to confound and delight me. It was only when the gallery owner invited me to meet Roger Muhl that some of the questions I had were answered.

In speaking about his artistic development, Muhl referred to a fellow artist who had taught him what to leave *out* of the canvas. I ventured, "Nicholas de Staal?" "Yes—Nicholas de Staal. How did you know?" "I felt it," I replied. "There is something in your work that reminds me of his but I couldn't put my finger on it until now."

When an artist leaves things *out* of his work, he allows the viewers to conjure up their own images, to make their own interpretations. The richer the possibilities, the deeper the enjoyment. The serendipity of meeting and becoming friends with Roger Muhl has taught me a great deal about life choices. Artists are always striving, ever assuming responsibility for everything they create. They seize art from

For art, there is no future, it's the living moment, then it's dead.

—PAUL BOCUSE

ordinary life, an idea, and mold it; the smallest variations and choices are critical. You don't own the art; it owns you.

Artist are free spirits, broad-minded and open, exercising the joy and exhilaration of play. They work in their studios day after day. Their work becomes a form of meditation. They work the clay, chisel the stone, mold the words—their activity is a combination of discipline, dedication, and inspired compulsion. They never take shortcuts because they understand and respect the orderliness of the process. It's work, but then again it isn't. Joseph Campbell understood that: "Work," he said, "begins when you don't like what you're doing."

Because the artist is in the flow of play, he or she becomes transported, transfixed, carried away by the creative experience. Artists also show deep respect, almost to the point of reverence, for the materials they use, learning through experimentation about their limits. After an intense burst of concentration comes the exhilaration. The mystery is touched with a bit of magic, and a work is finished. While an artist experiences the greatest happiness (and agony) in the process of creation, still he or she feels great satisfaction at the moment of standing back and examining something newly finished. The rewards are tangible. You can see, touch, feel, smell, and hear the work you've brought to life.

Artists often expect to fail. Failure is part of the process. It doesn't matter, it is part of learning. The artist loves to try, to experiment, to go through different periods and styles. Self-expression is key. A real artist always chooses new challenges and is never complacent. When something becomes easy, it no longer holds excitement. Every time an artist has a new exhibition or a concert or a new play or book, the work has to stand on its own. There's no resting on laurels. By the time the work is unveiled to the public, the artist has fulfilled the responsibility to his or her own conscience. One satisfies one's own heart first. This awareness of the importance of the work, of standing behind it no matter what the critics say, is a vital part of the creative act.

Life is change. Artists capture time by arresting and seizing the motion of life. Their mission is to have us see, taste, touch, smell, hear, and intuit life on a higher level. Their curiosity pushes them to remain open to unexpected experiences, to stay in touch and in tune with the times in which they live as well as their own inner self.

The artist believes in a vision. The artist is a channel for beauty which at its most sublime and transcendental level expresses a moral truth. The artist creates harmony — a glimpse of the divine.

THE ART OF LIVING

Choosing to live with the same sensitivity, integrity, and curiosity that characterize the best artists is what we can all do for ourselves now. The artist has a task that he or she feels as an obligation, and that is to remind us of our own humanity and potential for creativity. The art of living is the highest calling of all. If we start seeing our life as a work of art-in-progress, we will find that our attitude

You must learn day by day, year by year, to broaden your horizon. The more things you love, the more you are interested in, the more you enjoy, the more you are indignant about—the more you have left when anything happens.

—ETHEL BARRYMORE

toward our life will change and we will respect all our choices.

We can't live by intellect alone; we need inspiration as well as information. We will never know enough, and in fact we will die ignorant of many things, but if we choose to make an art of living, our lives will become an act of grace. Share joy by expressing yourself. Don't take any of your talents for granted. Use them, don't squander them. Regular use replenishes the spirit and creates order out of your experiences. When you create something original—a work of art, or your own artful life—you are building something that others can enjoy.

The artist transcends pain and suffering by embarking on this quest. Make living as an art your quest, your personal mission.

In order to find inspiration to nurture your vision, you need what Joseph Campbell calls "a sacred place." This is where you will find tranquility, where you will relish moments of rich solitude. In my earliest childhood, I would go to the hayloft in our red barn and lie down quietly, away from the busyness of our large, active family.

The other sacred place for me was first my mother's flower garden, and later, from age seven on, my own. Ever since, I have tried to help others understand the extraordinary importance of having one's own sanctuary. When my girls were little, I created a secret place on the top of their huge walk-in closet which they could reach by climbing on a ladder. Going to that magic place sent a signal that said it was private time—a rule we all respected.

As I recall all the sacred places that I have successfully helped my clients discover over the years, a strange situ-

Sacred space and sacred time and something joyous to do is all we need. Almost anything then becomes a continuous and increasing joy.

—JOSEPH CAMPBELL

ation I once came across comes to mind. An artist who was living in a town house with her husband, two sons, and a dog found it emotionally impossible to create her own place, a place where she could work. She had moved from a loft where she had a huge studio, but she had yet to unpack her canvases and paints. She used any excuse to avoid the issue—she even turned a spare upstairs room with a northern exposure into a sewing room.

I've never known an artist who couldn't figure out a way to work. When I asked Sally where she would paint, she replied, "I don't know. I'll move around the house," as though in afterthought. The fact that she was incapable of choosing a place to paint in made it clear to me that she was adrift. Sure enough, her paint tubes dried up and eventually her marriage did too. Once divorced, she went back to living in a loft where the studio became once more a priority.

It is a clear danger sign whenever any of us neglects the need for our own sacred space. "In your sacred space, things are working in terms of *your* dynamic," explains Campbell, "and not anybody else's. Your sacred space is where you can find yourself again and again."

Recently I had a fascinating conversation with Roger Muhl, whose paintings I've continued to collect for over thirty years. He told me that he has never *worked* a day in his life: He plays. "The most important thing in life" he said, "is to keep passion alive." "How?" I asked. "How do you refresh yourself?" Muhl answered, "I believe you must regularly get away from people. This is what works for me."

For me, a sacred place is somewhere I can go to pursue

some "field of action." It is a place to retreat to so I can deepen my consciousness. Campbell teaches us that "you can turn any place into a sacred space. . . . In a sacred space, everything is done so that the environment becomes a metaphor."

I have found innumerable such places even in crowded New York City. When I was working for Mrs. Brown, during my lunch breaks I would go light a candle in a cool, quiet church, or go to my favorite spot, the William Paley Park, where I'd get a refreshment and be soothed by the waterfall. Or I'd go to a museum garden to just sit and be still. Even Chock Full O'Nuts was a sacred place, a transition between home and office. I would have a cup of coffee and write a few lines before going to work. Hotel rooms, airplanes, even airports can serve this purpose. The rest of the world, the distractions to my right and left, are obliterated. Emerson teaches us that "the necessity of solitude is deeper . . . and is organic." Now, when I go to my writing study, five hours can go by with the swiftness of a good dream. When I awaken, I am surprised to discover what time it is.

Choose to set aside some time alone on a regular basis; it will put your life in perspective. What you do when you're utterly alone represents a pure choice about your life. The more we meditate, the calmer we become. When we feel without hope—that is the time to turn away from the daily bustle. That is when we need to restore balance. When we are continually on the go, giving away pieces of ourselves without taking time to replenish our spirits, we cannot feel the calm at the center that Joseph Campbell calls bliss.

The essence of all faith for people of my belief is that man's life can be, and will be, better.

—THOMAS WOLFE

The toughest choices require internal discipline, not one imposed from the outside. It is when we choose to dig deeper into ourselves—our nature, personality, character, and values—that we make useful discoveries about the meaning of our *own* life. When we lose the belief that we can make a difference, we must seek enlightenment, not give up.

Life would be a painful, drawn-out death sentence if we couldn't expand our inner selves by illuminating the darkness within. If we choose to strengthen our core resources, we will be less vulnerable to the manipulations of others. Choose or you'll be chosen.

In a troubled world, I am an optimist. I have consciously chosen to live as beautifully as possible in the time I have. I remember being on a holiday in St. Croix where it rained off and on for three days. A friend who was also vacationing there invited us to join him on his side of the island. When we told Hap that we hadn't been able to go to the beach since we'd arrived, he said, "Really? We've had sunshine every day." And sure enough, barely a few minutes from our hotel we drove into sunlight. I was taught a lesson: the sun is always shining somewhere.

When we're feeling hopeless, when we're going through a stressful, discouraging time, others, somewhere, are feeling joy. We all live ups and downs, highs and lows. We get our share of happiness and sadness, sun and rain, contentment and frustration, health and sickness.

Whether we are going through a sad period or a joyful one, we must remember that we can always choose to love. The word "love" has become trivialized, abused. And yet it is that deep feeling that when translated into generous

> I call heaven and earth to witness this day: I have put before you life and death, blessings and curse. Choose life — that you and your offspring shall live.
>
> —DEUTERONOMY

actions becomes the catalyst for opening doors and windows that let in light, energy, and music. So, I repeat, we can *choose* to love. Let us love ourselves out of sheer gratitude for existence. *Inner* contentment is where love originates and blossoms, and soars from. You awaken to the awesome reality that your sacred place could be a bench in the garden or a chair in your study; it can be anywhere, since it's always inside you.

Choose to recognize, live, and honor the expression of your inner self. When you love the process of creating something, you forget about your self-consciousness and become part of something bigger, more mysterious, more wonderful. Once you experience this illumination, you become transformed spiritually. The way you choose to raise children, spend your free time, the decisions you make about your family, your lifestyle, your career, your friends, your contributions to society, become a manifestation of a larger, more coherent whole because of your love of life.

The *Tao-te-ching*, the classic manual on the art of living, is referred to simply as *The Book of the Way*. The author, Lao-tzu, was a sage whose large-heartedness, humor, and wisdom grace every page. In the words of Stephen Mitchell, he teaches us that the true way is "to do by *not* doing, a paradigm for nonaction, the purest and most effective form of action. Less and less do you need to force things." Nothing is done, as it were, because the doer has wholly become one with the deed; the fuel has been completely transformed into the flame. This "nothing" is, in fact, "everything." Of all the great spiritual leaders, Lao-tzu is the most "female." We can embrace his perspective and enrich our lives and that of our children. Let go, and love will expand and blossom.

When Peter and I planned to marry, he told me that his family motto was "Learn to Die" (*Apprendre à mourir*). We talked about it and realized that it didn't suit us and that we should create our own. We decided on "Learn to Love," which we felt was more appropriate to the journey awaiting us. Death is not the emphasis; life is. And for us, life *is* love. Once we have loved fully, then we will be able to let go. Only then can we learn to die.

Nature can act as a guide, as it did for the Taoists. Feel the rhythms of the seasons in all their aspects. As summer fades into autumn, accept the change. Gradually, autumn (no matter how spectacular) leads to winter. Snow. Darkness. Death. But we always have the promise of spring, the metaphor for the renewal of life. All choices—good, bad, and mediocre—originate in you, and whenever you neglect yourself, you lose your ability to choose wisely. Choose to accept what comes your way—even tragedy—as necessary parts of life. Nothing lasts forever, neither winter nor spring.

You either let things happen or you choose to make things happen for you. Henry David Thoreau once said, "I would write about someone else if I knew anyone as well." Only you *know* yourself, and only I truly *know* me, thus my choices will be different from yours. I hope that as we make decisions for ourselves—be they simple or difficult—we will feel empowered by the ultimate truth that we always are free to choose.

The fourteenth-century mystic Julian of Norwich—

You don't get to choose how you're going to die. Or when. You can only decide how you're going to live. Now.

—JOAN BAEZ

221

named after the church of St. Julian—the first female writer in English, reassured us that we will be taken care of by a power greater than ourselves:

> "I shall make all things well,
> and I will make all things
> well and you will see yourself
> that every kind of thing will be
> well."